PREACHING THROUGH THE YEAR OF MARK

SERMONS THAT WORK VIII

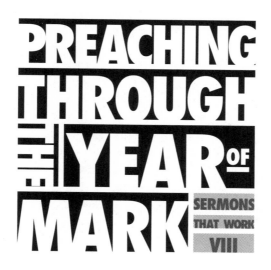

PREACHING THROUGH THE YEAR OF MARK

SERMONS THAT WORK VIII

Edited by
Roger Alling and David J. Schlafer

with a Foreword by
A. Gary Shilling

MOREHOUSE PUBLISHING

Morehouse Publishing
P.O. Box 1321
Harrisburg, PA   17105

Morehouse Publishing is a division of The Morehouse Group.

Printed in the United States of America

Cover design by Rick Snizik

Preaching through the year of Mark   :   sermons that work VIII /
   edited by Roger Alling and David J. Schlafer   ;
   with a foreword by A. Gary Shilling.
      p.   cm.
   Includes bibliographical references.
   ISBN 0-8192-1761-1 (pbk.)
      1. Episcopal Church—Sermons.   2. Sermons, American.
   3. Church year sermons.   I. Alling, Roger, 1933–   .
   II. Schlafer, David J., 1944–   .
   BX5937.A1P746   1999
   252'.03—dc21
                                                    99-28155
                                                    CIP

EDITORS

Roger Alling is President of the Episcopal Preaching Foundation, and Director of the Foundation's widely acclaimed Preaching Excellence Program for students in Episcopal seminaries. He has edited each of the eight volumes in *Sermons That Work*, this sermon anthology series committed to the celebration and nurture of preaching in the Episcopal tradition. He has been a parish priest and diocesan stewardship officer. Currently he serves as priest associate at parishes in the Dioceses of Central Pennsylvania and Southwest Florida.

David J. Schlafer is an independent consultant in homiletical formation. A former philosophy professor and seminary sub-dean, he has taught homiletics at four Episcopal seminaries and the College of Preachers. He leads preaching conferences in a variety of institutional and denominational settings in the United States, Canada, and England. He has coedited *Sermons That Work* since Volume V. He has written *Surviving the Sermon: A Guide to Preaching for Those Who Have to Listen, Your Way with God's Word: Discovering Your Distinctive Preaching Voice*, and *What Makes This Day Different?: Preaching Grace on Special Occasions.*

CONTENTS

3   Preaching Through Early Pentecost

4 Proclaiming in Late Pentecost

5 The Preacher as Theologian and Teacher

6 Proclamation in the Company of Preachers

FOREWORD

PREACHING is our passion—excellent preaching, that is. To reflect our mission of promoting and supporting excellent preaching in the Episcopal Church, we've changed our name from the Episcopal Evangelism Foundation to the Episcopal Preaching Foundation.

As you'll learn in the Introduction, we've also made another change. Earlier, we solicited sermons from all Episcopal parishes, which were judged by the directors of the Foundation in order to select the best to include in this annual volume. This year, however, we solicited and collected sermons related to the liturgical year "B," with gospels largely from Mark. Consequently, these sermons should be useful both to those in the pews and those in the pulpits as the next liturgical year "B" unfolds, starting November 28, 1999.

As in our previous seven sermon books, this one also contains the lectures and sermons delivered by the faculty and guests at our annual Preaching Excellence Program, held in Canton, Mississippi, in early June 1998. As in the past, the program included over fifty Episcopal seminarians who were selected by their seminary deans and preaching professors for their outstanding promise as preachers. They spent the usual intensive week on the art and practice of preaching, led by six homiletics professors and six skilled parish preachers.

The sermons from parishes from around the country were selected with great skill by our editors, the Reverend Roger Alling and the Reverend Dr. David J. Schlafer. I trust you agree that these sermons and the material from last summer's conference provide spiritually enriching and meaningful reading now and for the liturgical year to come.

Our Foundation is now in its twelfth year of promoting excellent preaching. I hope you've personally enjoyed some of the benefits of our efforts. Most of the five hundred-plus graduates of our conferences are actively preaching in parishes. Maybe one of them is in your midst. This book, like its seven predecessors, may reach many more lay people and clergy. If you haven't benefited so far, perhaps you will soon, starting with this book. In any event, Episcopal preaching still needs improvement. Please aid our efforts with your prayers, suggestions and tax-deductible contribution.

Dr. A. Gary Shilling
Chairman, The Episcopal Preaching Foundation, Inc.
500 Morris Avenue
Springfield, New Jersey 07081
973-467-0070
e-mail: shil@ix.netcom.com

INTRODUCTION

"The Time Is Now!"

IT DOESN'T take Jesus long to get his preaching life up and running in the Gospel of Mark. Eleven verses into the opening chapter, he is already going full steam. For a beginning preacher, his message is remarkably well focused and rather well plotted:

1. The time is fulfilled!
2. The Kingdom of God has come near!
3. Repent, and believe in the Good News!

Now, Jesus has probably had some help in his sermon preparation. Children learn to talk by listening in on the conversations of folks who are bigger than they are; and preachers learn to preach by hearing and responding to sermons. It doesn't take a world class biblical exegete to recognize the vigorous style and the straightforward substance of John the Baptist's preaching in the clarion call of Jesus that sets off the surging energy of Mark's Gospel.

And, of course, Jesus has had other homiletical resources upon which to draw as well. Other preaching models—a long line of them—have prepared the way for *him* to announce the imminent approach of God's inbreaking reign. Unless this line of prophets is simply a succession of supernatural fax machines, the preachers whom they have been inform the proclamation of Jesus as well.

No preacher simply begins to shape and share the Word in isolation. As Harry Pritchart once observed, "We all preach from somewhere in the midst of a procession." The Jesus shown to us in the Gospel of Mark is no exception. Previous preachers have had an impact, not just upon content of the Good News he proclaims, but also on its framing and its flavoring. Jesus has had help—quite competent help—in getting up to speed as a preacher of the gospel.

And yet, of course, there is a difference.

There always is.

No preacher can preach another's sermon. Some of us, on occasion, have been tempted to try. It never works. Part of what it means to be a preacher is to embody the Word afresh. To wrestle with the homiletical angel. To be personally wounded, named, and blessed by a personal encounter with the Word. And sent forth, in fear and trembling, to specific potential listeners in a particular, distinctive setting. The Good News is always the same; but if it is an authentic Word from the Lord, it never sounds exactly alike from one sermon to another.

But the preaching ministry of Jesus is distinguished from his predecessors by something more than his uniqueness—either as a unique human being or as a unique manifestation of God's universal love. There is an immediacy, an urgency. The pulse and pace of Mark's Gospel pick this up faithfully, and pass it on plainly. The translation of Mark 1:15 that appears in *Today's English Version* conveys the sense very well:

"The right time has come," [Jesus] said, "and the Kingdom of God is near! Turn away from your sins and believe the Good News!"

"The time is *now!*"

This is by no means the first time that a prophet of the Lord has preached with a sense of urgency. It is not the first time, nor will it be the last time, that "now" is announced as the "day of salvation." "The moment to decide" is one that, contrary to the sentiments of an oft-sung hymn, comes *more* than "once to every man and nation." Yet the hymn, written in the midst of America's agonizing conflict over slavery, has a point—there *are* decisive turning points— roads that diverge, and the choice of which to take (as Robert Frost says) "makes all the difference."

That kind of urgency animates Jesus' preaching acts in Mark's Gospel. Individuals, congregations, churches, and cultures may be brought to this critical point at different times, in different ways, and under different circumstances. But the urgency of the Word who is Jesus in the Gospel of Mark is a message both universal and unique: "The time is fulfilled; the time is now!" The turning point that Jesus announces, and embodies, is the crux on which the Kingdom turns. It is that toward which all other proclamation has pointed, and will point. The urgency is fresh, the immediacy relevant, whenever "The time is now" is sounded.

Preaching through the Year of Mark means more than following by rote the succession of steps that constitutes the liturgical game plan known as Lectionary Year B. Indeed, most of the sermons appearing in this volume—as most of the Scripture lessons appointed for this liturgical cycle—are drawn from other biblical sources. Preaching *through* Mark involves attempting to catch and convey, over the course of a preaching year, something of the tempo and thrust that is evident in the first and centering preaching words of Jesus with which Mark commences. The sermons that comprise this anthology are an attempt to foster such preaching, such listening, and such acting.

For readers who do not themselves regularly stand in the pulpit, but who participate in the preaching process from the pew, this collection is offered as further nourishment for spiritual journeys, and as healthy stimulus to responsible action in the face of God's imminently approaching reign. No matter how helpful the preaching you normally listen to may be, the simple, unequivocal call of Jesus can be—and needs to be—heard in new and different ways.

For those whose role in preaching is one of meeting the angel for a weekly homiletical wrestling match, this collection serves a complementary purpose. Obviously, the sermons here will not do your wrestling for you. For one thing, the limitations of space appropriate to a volume such as this dictate a sampling of Year B preaching occasions, rather than a complete compendium. What you read may even make your preaching preparation more extensive and demanding. Reading this sermon or that may make you say, "I need to incorporate her essential insight in my own way—but *how*?" or, "His approach compels me to think through my standard strategy again!" Or, "Certainly not *that*! But if that isn't the way to preach this text, then *what is?*"

Most important, however, is this: since, for many if not most preachers, preparing to preach is not only difficult but also lonely, the sermons in this volume may serve as a tangible, perhaps even almost audible reminder of the procession that surrounds you when you preach. It is a reminder of that chorus of witnesses who, along with you, are also doing their best to announce, as best they can, and in their own ways, the urgent word that "The time is now! The Kingdom is near!" Perhaps you can gain insight and courage from your preaching colleagues and realize anew that there are other ways of saying, "Repent and believe in the Good News!" than the way that has been given to you.

Those who have followed this sermon anthology series over the last seven years will immediately recognize a shift in the focus of this volume. What orchestrates it is not a homiletical theme, which has been the case for the last three years, but rather the liturgical year that will commence soon after its publication. With the generous support of Morehouse Publishing, and especially the highly professional assistance of editors Debra Farrington and Christine Finnegan, this plan projects analagous volumes to be issued for the next two years of the three-year liturgical cycle.

Another difference in this volume is the principle of selection. As a fuller expression of the collegial understanding of preaching to which the Episcopal Preaching Foundation is committed, the sermons included here are not the winners of a contest. The editors have tried to be deeply attentive to homiletical quality in the hard choices they have had to make. But they have listened for diversity of style and approach, as well as for excellence. And, of course, the primary consideration was to put together sermons appropriate for each season in the year and for many of the special liturgical occasions that punctuate the regular seasonal rhythm. In no way does lack of inclusion in this volume negatively reflect on scores of sermon offerings made by preachers from around the country. Although not explicitly, the voices of those preachers are a part of the chorus that is sounded in this volume.

One feature of previous volumes is continued here—sermons preached at the Preaching Excellence Conference that is offered each year for students in each of the Episcopal Church's eleven seminaries. The sermons re-presented here were delivered in June, 1998, at the well-appointed and well-managed Episcopal Diocesan Conference Center in Canton, Mississippi. As you will shortly learn, a sense of Mark's "The time is *now*!"—with respect to the urgency of the preaching vocation itself—energized every aspect of that conference. The unfolding homiletical conversation there, in the succession of sermons offered in the daily conference worship and in the theological analysis exemplified by Dr. McDaniel's lecture, was too helpful and too exciting to keep within the limits of the community that convened for the week. And so it is only appropriate to invite you into that conversation as well.

PREACHING THROUGH ADVENT, CHRISTMAS, AND EPIPHANY

SECOND SUNDAY IN ADVENT

Removing Dirt—Reversing Direction

Mark 1:1–18
Valerie A. Valle

IMAGINE that you've spent the evening at a friend's house somewhere east of Byron. When you leave to go home you discover that it is a dark and foggy night, so you get in your car and drive along, carefully following those little yellow dots that show where the middle of the highway is. You have been driving for quite a while, and your spouse sitting next to you is complaining that things don't look right—shouldn't there have been a turn back there? You mutter back something about backseat drivers and continue on. Now you are making a little better time, because there is a car in front of you. At least there are those two red lights to follow. You know nothing of the person driving that car, or where he is headed, but at least there is someone to follow.

Then, suddenly you see a strangely dressed man standing in the road holding a stop sign and waving and jumping up and down to get your attention. With hesitation, you stop and roll down the window just a little. "Turn around! You are going the wrong way!" he says. You look confused. "Turn around! If you keep going this way you will hurt yourself or someone else," he repeats. "But I'm being careful," you respond. "Turn around! The lights you are following belong to a drunk who could lead you off the road, who will lead you only to death!" he states with great drama. "Who are you and why should I trust you?" you ask. "Turn around," he keeps saying.

Finally he brings out a bucket of water and pours it over your windshield. To your surprise, it is no longer foggy outside. What you had thought was fog was really all the dirt on your own windshield. As you can see outside, you realize that you are very far from home, you have no idea how many hours you were going the wrong direction, and it dawns on you that you are totally lost. You also notice that the car you were following is about to go off into a ditch. You turn to the man beside you to thank him and ask him how to get home. "Follow that one over there," he says as he points to a light in the distance. As you pull away you ask your spouse, "Who was that?" "Oh, I think he was a workman preparing the road, making the highway in this desert straight."

John the Baptizer proclaimed a baptism of repentance for the forgiveness of sins. Repentance? What is repentance? The word is a translation of *metanoia*, a Greek word that means to know again in a new way, to be transformed, to turn around. When someone calls for repentance they are telling you to turn around. To turn around because you are going in the wrong direction. To turn around so that you can see things in a new way. A baptism of repentance would be a baptism that provides one an opportunity to see things in a new way.

How much of our lives we spend as if we were wandering lost in the fog! We have no sense of where we are going, we don't see the dangers ahead, and sometimes we follow without knowing where this way will lead. How many of us wake up one morning and begin to question what we are doing with our lives? We follow a path set before us—school, marriage, job, whatever—without thinking about whether it leads to where we really need to go.

Perhaps you seek wealth, money for its own sake, without thinking about why you should be trying to get rich. And then you find, once you have some money, that you still feel empty inside. Perhaps it is power you follow after. Perhaps it is the dream of your own home and that fantasy middle-class life. Once you have achieved it, then what?

Maybe you have a gone down a road of addiction to alcohol or drugs and one day woke up to realize that this road leads nowhere. Maybe you idealized someone and followed him or her until you found that you had lost your own sense of identity.

Any time we make anything more important than God, more important than loving God and our neighbors, we are going in the wrong direction; sooner or later we find ourselves lost and at a dead end.

When we discover we have gone the wrong way there is only one thing to do—turn around. To repent, to turn around, means to acknowledge that we have been going the wrong way, to acknowledge that we have done things we should not have done, and not done things we should have done. To repent of our sins means to open our eyes and to acknowledge the mistakes we have made. To see ourselves in a new way, to acknowledge that we are lost, and to turn around. And to follow the One for whom John was preparing, to follow the true light that can lead us home.

Advent is a season with two themes. The first is the joyful anticipation of the birth of Christ, the incarnation of our Lord. The second is the preparing for the second coming of Christ. Both involve a sense of preparation, of self-study, so that we are ready to receive the incredible grace that God bestowed upon the earth on the first Christmas. We need to prepare to be able to let in how much God loves us. We need to be prepared to open our hearts and to receive the gift of love that is the Christ child.

How do we prepare? By opening our eyes and hearts, by allowing the dirt of our past that keeps us from seeing the truth to be washed away, by repenting and letting ourselves be transformed, so that when we see the true light we are ready to follow Christ home.

Valerie A. Valle is Vicar of St. Alban's Church, Brentwood, California.

FOURTH SUNDAY IN ADVENT

"How Can This Be?"
The Annunciation of Desire

Luke 1:26–38
Elizabeth Kaeton

I HAVE a wonderful friend who, like most of my good friends, is so unlike me that it might seem unlikely we would *be* friends. She's a long-distance runner, for one thing, while I struggle to remember to get in twenty to thirty minutes of exercise *daily*—er, um—*every other day*—okay, *weekly*! She's also a celibate Roman Catholic nun—not exactly my calling in life. Her birth name is Bonnie, but she is known as "Gabe"—short for her professed name of Sister Gabriel.

Gabe and I have had many long talks about religious life, spirituality, my curiosity concerning her life as a celibate woman, and her curiosity about my being a woman and a priest. Our longest-running conversation, however, has to do with the nature of prayer. After many conversations taking us long into the night, we have both come to an understanding about prayer—or so I thought. Imagine my surprise, then, when she came into the office last week, in total exasperation, and demanded, "Am I giving off vibes or something?"

She went on to report that several times in the past few days, while visiting her AIDS clients in their homes, young adolescent boys had made it known to her that they found her—well, I guess the polite term is "attractive." Enough to make what used to be referred to as "overtures." Her last experience with two preadolescent boys had pushed her over the edge.

"So, I'm in the elevator," said Gabe, "when these two kids around eleven or twelve get in on the eighth floor. I'm standing there, *in* my habit and *with* my escort, and they start giving me the once-over. One of the kids turns to me and says, 'Hey, because you're a nun, does that mean you can't have sex?'

"'Well,' I say, 'of course I *can* have sex. I just choose *not* to.'

"Just as I am silently congratulating myself on my response, one of the kids looks at me again—with *that* look, you know—and, shaking his head with a sadness beyond the knowing of his tender years, says, 'Hmmmm—too bad!'"

"So," demanded Gabe, "what is it? Am I giving off vibes or something?"
"Of course, you're giving off vibes, Gabe!" I answered. "But, how can that be? I'm a *celibate* Roman Catholic *nun*, for God's sake! I *can't* give off vibes!" she laughed. "I'll be excommunicated!"

And Mary said to the angel Gabriel, "But how can this be?"

I've been thinking a great deal lately about the nature of prayer and the nature of desire. Indeed, it has become a central part of my Advent meditations, and I've found strands of these themes weaving their way into more and more of my sermons. I find my conversations with my spiritual director sprinkled with references to sexuality and spirituality. How can this be?

Sexuality has become its own national religion. We've become totally obsessed with sex. Think of what captures the headlines: The sexual shenanigans of sportscaster Marv Albert. Lieutenant Kelly Flynn becomes the first woman in history to make fighter pilot status, only to be disgracefully discharged from the Air Force for "the oldest sin in history." And, thanks to the secretary from Arkansas, Paula Jones, we now know more about the sexual proclivities of our president than any other previous commander in chief.

I submit that this obsession with sex is just the surface of a deeper longing to know about intimacy, to know about desire and longing. It's easier to talk about sex, and to peer into the inner workings of other people's bedrooms, than it is to explore the boundaries of our own wilderness, our own desires, and our own fantasies.

Meanwhile, Bishop Spong, in the New Dimensions Lecture series, reports his belief that, in a culture that has accepted the demise of theism, traditional forms of prayer have no relevance. While I agree with Jack Spong on the later part of his thesis, I am not so pessimistic as to accept the first part: I do not believe that our culture has accepted the demise of theism. I don't think people believe that God is dead or that belief in God is passé or irrelevant.

I think we are understandably confused about the nature of God. Bobbi McCaughey, the mother of the recently born septuplets, captured this confusion in her statement about "selective reduction"—the now common procedure in multiple pregnancies of aborting some of the fetuses so that the remaining ones might have a better survival rate. "Oh," she said, her voice filled with almost stereotypical Midwestern naïveté, "we would *never* interfere with God's will!" This from a woman who had conceived those multiple pregnancies only by the grace of the scientific miracle of fertility drugs!

And Mary said to the angel Gabriel, "But how can this be?"

How can it be that we can clone a sheep in a petri dish, but we still can't predict the advent of a tornado? How can it be that God allows us the power to re-create life in a laboratory, but also stands by and allows the senseless and tragic destruction of life? Who is this God and what does God want in our lives? What might we want from God in our lives?

These two questions define the time we call Advent: What does God want in our lives? What might we want from God in our lives? The operative word in both queries is one that begins to hint at the nature of prayer: *Want. Desire. Longing.*

What do we desire most? What is the rapture of God? What is our deepest longing? What is God's most ardent passion? These are, essentially, questions of prayer.

The one thing I can say with certainty about my friend Gabe is that she is a person of prayer. As a person of prayer, she knows, in her deepest intuitive place of knowing, about desire. And so, it is no surprise to me that she is "giving off vibes." It's also no surprise to those of us who know anything about adolescents that they'd be the first to pick up on those vibes.

Even the prophet Isaiah alludes to desire and longing as an essential part of the relationship between God and humankind:

I joyfully exult in Yahweh; my soul delights in my God. For Yahweh has clothed me in garments of salvation, and arrayed me in a robe of righteousness—as a bridegroom puts on a crown, and a bride adorns herself with jewels.[1]

If you pardon the heterocentric imagery, guess what the bride and the bridegroom have, first and foremost, on their minds? A hint: it's not about garments of salvation and robes of righteousness! No, it's about that which gives *joy* and *delight*.

I want to tell you about joy, delight, intimacy, and desire from my own experience, a story about the first time I had the privilege of presiding at Eucharist. It's not an easy story to tell. It places me in peril of being dismissed as a mystic or a loon. Such is often the lot of people who speak of their desire for God, or of God's desire for them. Then again, I don't know any place where I might have the confidence to tell this story other than here in this community of faith.

It was October 19, 1986, the day after my ordination to the priesthood, and the first time I would preside at solemn sung Eucharist at St. John the Evangelist Church on Bowdoin Street in Boston. I have never learned to read music, so the notes on the page meant absolutely nothing to me, except to serve to guide me up or down the musical scale. Truth be told, my anxiety level was so high I couldn't read the *words* on the page. I was chanting this ancient love song from memory, from a place in me that existed from before time.

On my left stood the subdeacon, John, one of the kindest and gentlest souls God ever created. On my right stood the priest-as-deacon, Margaret, who had been a mentor and role model for what it meant to be a strong woman ordained to leadership. I don't remember much of the experience of *being* in the Eucharistic moment, except to say that it was awe-full, and filled with grace and power. I remember that, like some wonderful angelic chorus, John would prompt me with a gentle, loving reminder: "Easy. Easy. Go slow, now. Easy." And Margaret would occasionally chime in, "Relax. Breathe. You're doing fine."

After mass was over, we returned to the sacristy for final prayer. I remember collapsing in deep, uncontrollable sobs onto my knees on the floor of the sacristy, much to the surprise of everyone there—including me! Never had I felt more vulnerable or more naked. The rector, Emmett, not known for his tolerance of things emotional, seemed to know intuitively what to do. He knelt over me, taking his cope and surrounding me with the most holy embrace I have ever experienced. I can still feel the warmth of his face on my wet tears, and I can hear his breath as if it were the very breath of God.

"Tell me," he said gently, softly, more a request than a demand. "Tell me what you are feeling in this moment." And I, not exactly known for being at a loss for words, stumbled and stammered my answer. "I feel," I said, "as if I have just made love with God and it has been my joy and my delight to say to God's people, 'Come. Taste and see the goodness of our God.'"

Feeling even more foolish, I collapsed again into sobs. But Emmett seemed to know. He seemed to understand. "Ah," he said, "that is absolutely right. Never forget this feeling, my love. This is what you are called to do. You are to make love with God and invite all of God's people to do the same in their own way and in their own lives and at their own sacred tables." He held me close and whispered, "It *is* about *making . . . love*. It always has been. So shall it always be."

What would happen, do you suppose, if, instead of thinking of prayer as some safe, ritualized pattern of speech prescribed for you by learned men and women, you began to think of prayer as your deepest longing? What would happen, do you think, if you considered prayer as an expression of intimacy and desire—that of *your own for God* and that of *God's for you*?

What if you considered your most intimate relationship as a reflection of your relationship with God? What if you saw in your relationship with God a reflection of your most intimate relationship?

What if your deepest longing is *exactly* God's will for you?

And Mary asked, "How can this be?"

I want to suggest that, if you do nothing else with what's left of this Advent, you take Mary's question as your Advent prayer. I want to suggest that you ask God this question at least daily in Advent. "*How can this be?*" might just be the prayer that leads you to the heart of God, and the desire of God, and the longing of God. It might just be the prayer that leads you to your own heart, to your own desire, to your own longing.

Consider the angel Gabriel's response to Mary's question:

The Holy Spirit will come upon you, and the power of the Most High will overshadow you. . . . For nothing will be impossible with God.[2]

We, like Mary, will ask, "How can this be?" And God's love in Christ will be born to us in our own time, in our own day, and in our own way.

Elizabeth Kaeton is Canon Missioner in the Diocese of Newark.

---

1. Isaiah 61:10.
2. Luke 1:35a, 37.

CHRISTMAS DAY

The Doorway of the Nativity

Luke 2:1–20
Jennifer Phillips

ON THIS DAY, God has opened for us a little door into heaven itself, a door that shall never again be closed. Alleluia! Through it angels have come singing. Through it shepherds have glimpsed light arrowing through the sky. Through it the whole universe has passed in transformation into something new and shining: heaven has lit the earth, which glows with sacred fire. Nothing is as it was before.

We in the West envision the stable as a little building of wood or stone, but the old tradition of the East, recalled in all its Christmas iconography, is of a cave in the rock where beasts were stabled. In those images the Christ child has opened the womb of the earth, and all creation becomes newly fruitful in the re-creation of the One called Second Adam. The stone trough in which the swaddled babe is laid is a small coffin overlooked by the mild-faced ox and ass and ranks of stooping angels. And we are reminded at once of that other door in the earth through which Jesus passed into the resurrection, the door of a new-hewn tomb in the rock from which a stone was rolled away, opening to us the portal to our own eternal life.

In one strange icon of the Nativity by a follower of the fourteenth-century Russian painter Andrei Rubliev, the doorway of the cave in which the baby is entombed, as it were, is black. It is opaque behind the heads of the beasts, like a moonless, hidden landscape in the interior of the mountain. The baby swaddled like Lazarus in his grave clothes seems to be staring back into the darkness of the cave, away from the light and activity of the world outside. He seems regretful of leaving the place he had been before.

In one corner, wise men travel in haste on horseback, still a distance off. In another, baffled shepherds trudge up the hillside, their eyes fixed on a rather small star. In a lower corner two midwives are washing the newborn in a round font. Mary, a huge dark form, lies propped on her elbow, on a blood-red pallet half across the doorway of the cave. Her back is to the baby. She leans on her hand, shrouded in a long black garment; her face turned down, she is a picture of postpartum weariness, even depression.

Most curious of all, in the lower left Joseph sits by himself, old and dejected behind some stones. His chin is in his hand, while a fur-clad figure like a demon of temptation towers over him—raising, we may guess, a lot of ugly questions about the baby and the woman to whom he is betrothed. This nativity is unsettling, with its hints of exhaustion, discouragement, separation, arduous toil, and even darkness and death. The image reminds us that the doorway through which God comes into flesh is the doorway into the way of the cross and the tomb. The flesh and creation that are sanctified by God's coming among us are also heir to suffering, alienation, and difficulty for Jesus, as for us. This season brings human suffering into sharp relief against the light and joy we expect, but do not always find in it. This seems the icon of our human condition, the Holy Family not yet cohering, light not yet breaking forth from the birth; but the mystery nevertheless opening a doorway into something beyond.

"We seek what is beyond us, but our desire remains baffled," suggests Anglican theologian Donald Allchin. "We are thrown back on ourselves by the enigmas of sin and suffering, of frustration and death. Of ourselves we cannot attain the goal for which we long. It is only when another comes out from the unknown world of eternity to meet us, and opens to us the way through, that we can find fulfillment of the desire which we know within ourselves. In Christ, God, Godself comes out to meet us and becomes the way which leads into the Kingdom of heaven."[1]

The Welsh poet R.S. Thomas reflects on the Nativity through the same awareness of the linked doorways of birth and death:

> And God held in his hand
> A small globe. Look, he said.
> The son looked. Far off,
> As through water, he saw
> A scorched land of fierce
> Colour. The light burned
> There; crusted buildings
> Cast their shadows: a bright
> Serpent, a river
> Uncoiled itself, radiant
> With slime.
> On a bare
> Hill a bare tree saddened
> The sky. Many people
> Held out their thin arms
> To it, as though waiting
> For a vanished April
> To return to its crossed
> Boughs. The son watched
> Them. Let me go there, he said.[2]

The former bishop of Alaska, a member of the Choctaw Nation, published a wonderful Christmas meditation on the *kiva*, an underground chamber built by native tribes for religious ceremony and retreat. Many tribes believed that life emerged from within the womb of the earth into the human world, and that descending into the earth brought people back to that birthing place of hope and life. Bishop Charleston wrote: "I spent last Christmas in a kiva. At the time, of course, I didn't realize it. Only now, looking back over my shoulder, can I see the path that brought me there and then led me up again into the light.

"Like so many others for whom a holiday becomes a lament, I found myself out of sync with time, trapped between the season of joy and the reality of sorrow. Instead of feeling the warmth and happiness of the Christmas spirit, I was sleepwalking in the hypnosis of a private pain that kept me isolated from shopping malls and office parties. Like so many people do when they are hurting, I went underground." There, he found, "The isolation can become stillness. The dark can become comfort. The silence can become thought. The memories can become pathways. The pain can become passion. The loss can become hope. The denial can become truth. The weakness, strength. The empty places, open places waiting to be filled. The silent room a sacred place, a personal place, with just enough room for you and God to begin life again. . . . It is the gift of a true Christmas, one that does not ask you to come up to find it, but that comes down to find you."[3]

The cave in the rock is the doorway to the kiva, sacred place of beginning anew, the crucible of transformation: tomb, womb, and font of life. Step fearlessly down the long ladder to the manger-side of mystery. Meet the Christ child there.

Into the longing arms of the world, into your arms too, God has chosen to come, and not with pomp and power but with innocence and need like any one of us. That doorway of the Nativity through which we are invited to pass into new life is a small, person-sized opening. Small as the birth canal, or the bowl of the font of baptism. Small as a cave to shelter a few household animals, or a tomb into which one must stoop to enter. It is small enough to be overlooked by those without eyes to see the Epiphany-light of a star; and yet it is the doorway of all our possibility. Because Jesus has passed through it in coming to meet us, we also shall pass through on our way into the heart of God.

The little child invites us also to open the doors of our hearts to him. See, he is bound and helpless; waiting for you to offer the strength of your arms, your love, and your hope. Wouldn't you like to hold him? Yet he is also the radiant one, coming to us from eternity to draw us along with him into the mystery of new birth, a mystery of endless power and promise. See, he has opened for us a door. Nothing is as it was before. An angel sits on a stone and watches the entrance. Would you like to stoop down and go through into the mystery your heart desires?

Jennifer Phillips is Rector of Trinity Parish, St. Louis, Missouri.

---

1. Donald Allchin: *Participation in God* (Wilton, Connecticut: Morehouse-Barlow, 1988), 11.

2. *Poems of R. S. Thomas* (Fayetteville, Arkansas: University of Arkansas Press, 1985), 82–83. Reprinted by permission of the University of Arkansas Press. © 1992 by R. S. Thomas.

3. The Rt. Rev. Stephen Charleston, "A Christmas Gift from Native America," *Episcopal Life* (December 1996):16.

FEAST OF THE EPIPHANY

Displaced Persons

Matthew 2:1–15
David J. Schlafer

CAN YOU think of a time when you felt out of place? That isn't the same thing as being away from home.

A needed vacation, a changing vocation—these can take us to new, strange, even scary places. But coping with a *different* place is not the same thing as feeling out of place. It is, in fact, quite possible to find yourself out of place without even leaving home:

Older kids come over to play with your big sister, and suddenly you don't have a playmate anymore.

You come into a room where people are huddled in earnest conversation. Everyone suddenly stops talking and looks up at you with NO TRESPASSING signs on their faces.

You go back to your alma mater for a class reunion. All your old classmates have made a success of interesting careers. You are stuck in a job that is going nowhere.

The circumstances can vary widely, but the feeling is the same: *I really don't belong here. I am out of place.*

What is it that makes the difference between *strange* territory and *alien* territory? It's not so much the place as the people you find there. A fascinating new world can go suddenly flat if you are greeted with uninviting stares. On the other hand, the cold inscrutability of unfamiliar surroundings can instantly melt if you are met with a warm word of welcome. Part of what often encourages us to venture away from home, in fact, is the belief—or at least the hope—that we will find a word of welcome when we come at last to journey's end.

Today we hear a story about some folks who do leave home and venture into a far country. A star that they follow sparks within them the strong impression that they will find a welcome in the land toward which they are heading.

Wrong! So much for putting your trust in stars!

The wise men stand around in Herod's palace feeling decidedly out of place. The formal courtesies—they create a chasm. The interest in their mission—it is feigned, forced, and palpably hostile. This is not what the wise men left home to find.

But—cut the king some slack, will you? His Majesty himself feels out of place. This unexpected visit only underscores the anxiety Herod surely feels already. Being a king is not all it's cracked up to be. Uneasy is the head that wears the crown. And Herod's head is uneasier than most. Is Herod selfish? *Yes!* Cruel? *Definitely!* Is he in power? *That all depends on what you mean by "power."* Does he have cause to be uneasy? *Absolutely!* Rome is not an easy-going overlord. Judea is not an easily ruled underling. Herod's home is a throne on which he does not fit. Herod is a man who is utterly out of place.

Small wonder that he makes everyone around him feel the same. And small wonder that, in the presence of the wise men, the royal court feels as out of place as it makes the wise men feel.

Well! Nothing for them to do but pack it up and head on out. This is obviously a dead end. They might as well go back to where they came from. They probably should never have left home in the first place.

But "NO!" the star says. "NO!" And it proceeds to shine them toward the Welcome they have come all this way to worship.

Do they receive the welcome that they came for? *Of course they do! I should hope they would! Who in their right minds would turn away visitors bearing gifts?*

On Super Bowl Sunday, Publisher's Clearing House will send out its Prize Patrol again. To one lucky individual, the Prize Patrol will offer gifts of flowers, balloons, and a gigantic check for millions upon millions of dollars. Do you imagine for one minute that the person whose name appears upon the check will slam the door in the faces of the Prize Patrol?

Why shouldn't the Holy Family welcome the wise men with open arms? Gold, frankincense, myrrh—these are expensive gifts!

Yes, the gifts are expensive, all right—and perhaps not only in the way that comes most naturally to mind. The gifts that these visitors bring come with a cost—a cost that far exceeds the bane of unwanted publicity and high taxes— a cost of which those who bring the gifts probably have little inkling. But a cost, I suspect, that the family who receives them has already begun to sense.

I cannot think that the urgent call to head for Egypt, which comes to Joseph after the wise men leave, descends upon him as a total surprise. Joseph and Mary already know what it is to be displaced. Yet here is the irony of it all: it is the displaced persons who give the wise men welcome. To all external observations, if anyone should feel at home, Herod should. If anyone should feel out of place, the Holy Family should. And yet things are exactly the reverse of what it seems that they should be.

This story Matthew's Gospel tells us vividly prefigures the life and ministry of the One whom the wise men come to worship. One who shares food and healing with others, regardless of their sex, race, social status, religious affiliation, or political allegiance—even though he himself (as Matthew has him tell us later) has nowhere to lay his head. Another gospel writer puts it this way: the Word Made Flesh pitches his tent with the whole of humanity, but is not received when he comes unto his own.

Interesting, is it not, how those who know what it's like to be displaced are often the ones who are most adept at making others welcome? And those who cling for dear life to places they cannot hope to hold are the ones who inflict on others their own sense of profound dis-ease. The moves folks make in power games are almost always ploys to seize and secure a place that is forever slipping through their fingers.

Today we celebrate a very different kind of move—a move in which the Lord of life does not cling to the rightful prerogatives of position, but gives them up, so that all who have been made to feel out of place are freed to find, in him, a welcome.

And if this welcome is as wide as it claims to be, then even the Herods in our own hearts will no longer have to clutch their shaky thrones, because those thrones are as unnecessary as they are insecure. We come to Jesus as we are, with whatever gifts we have; and he spares no expense to make us welcome. That is a Welcome worth leaving home to find. That is a Welcome worth leaving home to share.

David J. Schlafer is coeditor of this volume.

FOURTH SUNDAY AFTER THE EPIPHANY

Where Is Epiphany Taking Us?

Mark 1:21–28
Scott C. Lee

I ONCE HAD a conversation with a friend who teaches church school in another congregation. Her job is to organize activities for young people that focus on the seasons of the church's year. "I understand Advent," she said. "I know what's going on there—and what is going to happen. And Lent, that's an easy one to deal with. Lent and Easter are so full of images and meaning and things to do. Even Pentecost; the kids can really get into thinking about wind and fire, the birthday of the church, and God's Spirit in the world. But," she said, "Epiphany? I just don't have a hold on Epiphany. It's not quite clear to me what it's all about."

I expect my friend is not alone in this, so I want to look at where we are in the church's year . . . and how we got here. Epiphany is a word that means "manifestation," or "showing," and it is a season of the church's year that addresses the question posed in the ancient carol—"What Child is this . . . ?" or more accurately, "Who is this man that the Christmas child has become?" It is a season that progressively reveals who Jesus is.

On the day of Epiphany, almost four weeks ago, we saw the magi, wise men from the east, bringing gifts to the baby Jesus. We learn from them that this child is more special than we could possibly imagine. They tell us that this child is important not only to Israel, but that he is a person of global, universal importance. At Jesus' baptism, which we celebrate just after the day of Epiphany, John says that this man Jesus is the One whom he and all the prophets have foretold; the One God had promised. We learn at the baptism that the Spirit of God is with Jesus in a new and powerful way. And after his baptism, Jesus becomes an itinerant preacher who gathers about him a group of followers as he moves about the countryside. Nathaniel and Philip. Simon and Andrew. James and John. Then we hear how he looked at them and said, "Repent, drop what you are doing, turn around. Follow me."

And today we are in Capernaum, standing in a synagogue with Simon, Nathaniel, and the others, following and listening to this remarkable man Jesus; not quite sure who he is or what he is going to do. Wondering, like my friend, "What's it all about? What is going to happen? What difference will he make? What is he going to do?"

Mark tells us that one of the things Jesus did was to teach. And he taught in a new way the teaching to which they were accustomed. Jesus spoke somehow with authority. The scribes, the teachers of the law, relied on elaborate and impressive arguments to make their points—arguments based on quotations from the Scriptures. Jesus himself quoted Scripture to illuminate his teaching. But, unlike the scribes, Jesus spoke with an authority of his own—not in opposition to, but not derived from quoting the Scriptures. He taught with an authority of his own.

God promised Israel that he would raise up teachers and prophets for them. Prophets to bring them God's Word. Prophets to speak for God to God's people. And now Jesus stands in the line of these prophets. He speaks God's Word to God's people. But Mark wants to tell us that Jesus was greater even than the prophets. Jesus' teaching is coupled with action. His words are effective. He is even able, Mark tells, to cast out demons.

What are we to make of this reference to "demons"? We may or may not share the understanding of the world that prevailed in New Testament times: that there are in the world evil spirits, powers with a life and ungodly energy of their own. But I can speak from my own experience, and from my awareness of the lives of others, that the forces that enslave us, that compel us to hurtful and selfish behavior, are quite real and active still. Have you seen anger so powerful that it seemed to take on a life of its own? Do you know of a disagreement that began in the family, at the office, or in the church, perhaps around a significant issue, which quickly grew into fearful conflict between opposing factions? A conflict that seemed to grow larger than the issue, to feed itself and grow by its own heat?

Twelve-step programs like AA and Gamblers Anonymous begin their grace-filled healing by asking members to recognize that there is an enslaving force in their lives over which they are powerless. Today's Gospel treats these powers as real, and it uses their reality to tell us who Jesus is. He has power and authority over whatever would enslave us and damage our relationship with God.

That is the point of Mark's story. Jesus brings into our lives the power and the authority to set us free and bring us into union with God.

Those who stood around him in the synagogue were amazed, and they wondered what it could mean. They remind me of my friend who was wondering about the meaning of Epiphany: the wonder and the amazement are real, but the answers are so far incomplete. Even Mark, who tells us here that Jesus taught in the synagogue, does not indicate what was the content of that teaching. Mark knew that no synopsis of the course was possible.

The claims being made about Jesus, in this lesson and throughout this season, are not here being given their fullest, most complete expression. The full statement of who Jesus is will be made later in the Gospel. Through this story of Jesus' teaching and casting out an evil spirit, Mark tells us that Jesus is the Holy One of God, the One who brings freedom and wholeness.

It is, however, not in exorcism or teaching that we see most clearly who Jesus is. It is in the cross. We stand today with those first followers in the synagogue, ready to follow this itinerant preacher as he reveals to us once more who he is. Once more, we have the opportunity to spend the days and weeks ahead listening to his teaching, watching our lives and the lives of those around us for the effects of his power. We already know where that following will lead us. It will lead us to the cross . . . and beyond.

But it is important for us to retrace the path, to experience the revelation again, to hear the words again, to hear them again for the first time. Because the gift he has to give us, the teaching he would have us hear, the freedom he would lead us to is deeper and broader, and more graceful and lovely than we have yet imagined. And even the road to the cross is the way of life and peace.

Epiphany is a time to recommit ourselves to the journey. To acknowledge the questions. To admit the confusion and doubt. And to join with the other disciples, those who are gathered in this room with us, making once again the decision to follow Jesus, to the cross and beyond.

Scott C. Lee is Rector of St. Mark's Church in Antioch, Tennessee.

LAST SUNDAY AFTER THE EPIPHANY

The Transfiguration As a Model of Religious Experience

2 Peter 1:16–19; Mark 9:2–9
Nancy A. Willis

HERE IT IS, the Sunday before the beginning of Lent, the penitential season that invites us into the wilderness—perhaps to wrestle with our demons, to become more aware of our sinfulness, to undertake a spiritual discipline for our soul's health, to seek forgiveness, to attempt some amendment of life. But before embarking on that spiritual journey, the Epiphany season takes us on a different route up the mountain. This "mountaintop experience" is a revelatory manifestation of a divine being—the transfiguration of Jesus Christ. The transfiguration can be a model for us of "peak" experiences, encounters with Christ, encounters with the divine.

Like the Old Testament theophanies in which God appeared to Moses and Elijah, the transfiguration is an extraordinary event shrouded in mystery. According to the book of Exodus, God hid Moses in the cleft of a rock and covered him, so that he would see only God's back after God passed by. The effect of this experience, and of Moses' conversations with God in the cloud or in the tent of meeting, was obvious. The Scripture tells us, "When Aaron and all the Israelites saw Moses, the skin of his face was shining, and they were afraid to come near him." From then on Moses covered his face with a veil after he had been talking with God to protect the Israelites from the alarming sight of his shining face. A cloud, a tent, a radiant appearance too bright to look upon—these are elements of the transfiguration story that link it with the Hebrew covenant, and, perhaps, give both the Jewish disciples and the earliest Christians who preserved the story a context for understanding their experience. What might these images mean for us?

Initially there is the extraordinary vision, the transfigured Jesus whose appearance is so radiant that only his clothes can be described—"dazzling white, such as no one on earth could bleach them." We may want to say to Mark, "Is that all you can tell us? Surely there is more to say about Jesus on the mountaintop." Well, maybe not. We, too, have had experiences that defy description, experiences that are beyond words. We must be satisfied with "dazzling white" clothes, although we know that the description is partial and suggestive rather than definitive.

Then Elijah and Moses, who had their own mountaintop experiences of God, appear in conversation with Jesus. Such a vision and encounter would leave most of us tongue-tied, but the ever-impetuous Peter speaks up: "Rabbi, it is good for us to be here; let us make three dwellings: one for you, one for Moses, and one for Elijah." Mark adds, to Peter's credit, "He did not know what to say, for they were terrified." In Peter's suggestion to build dwellings, probably tents, there is a frequently encountered pitfall—one that is easy to understand, granted Peter's awe-inspired confusion.

The desire to build three dwellings can be an attempt to prolong the experience, to stay on the mountain, isolated from the flow of life—in this case to remain in the glory of divine presence without having to follow the way of the cross. Building the dwellings would be like trying to freeze-frame an experience. It can be done in art, but not in life.

John Keats in one of his odes describes the scenes depicted on a Grecian urn as moments frozen in time. Of the lover pursuing his beloved, he says:

> *Bold Lover, never, never canst thou kiss,*
> *Though winning near the goal—yet, do not grieve;*
> *She cannot fade, though thou hast not thy bliss,*
> *For ever wilt thou love, and she be fair!*

These lovers never age, their ardor never dims, but their love is never consummated. What is *fine* in a work of art is, in life, *death.*

In Charles Dickens's novel, *Great Expectations*, Miss Haversham has been deserted by her betrothed on their wedding day. She spends the rest of her life sitting in the darkened reception room. Wrinkled and gray, she sits in her ragged wedding gown beside the banquet table laden with crumbled, moldy food draped in cobwebs. Life is a long course of moments—some sublime and some horrible. We cannot freeze-frame or build dwellings for any of them, the best or the worst.

Though outwardly a sign of respect for Jesus, Moses, and Elijah, Peter's desire to build dwellings may also be an attempt, be it ever so subtle or even unconscious, to control the situation. We like to be in control of our lives and our environment by putting things in containers, drawing boundaries, classifying, and categorizing. The spiritual experience defies control. It is not a possession, but rather by it we are possessed by God. The disciples followed where Jesus led them. They followed him up the mountain to witness the transfiguration, an awesome experience.

And the sheer awe of the experience excuses Peter's impetuosity, his impulse to preserve and to control the situation. "He did not know what to say, for they were terrified." Peter, James, and John are feeling that paradoxical combination of fear and fascination that characterizes the religious experience, the mixed emotion of awe. They are terrified, yet they cannot tear themselves away.

I have captured this emotion in a snapshot of my daughter at age two, watching workmen break up our street with pneumatic drills. She is covering her face with her hands, but her separated fingers reveal a wide-eyed stare. She is terrified, but she cannot look away. For a two-year-old, the deafening noise of the drills and the apparent destruction of a piece of her stable world are awesome.

For the disciples the overshadowing of a cloud transposes the awesome moment. A voice emerges: "This is my Son, the Beloved; listen to him!" The divine message is reminiscent of that which Jesus heard at his baptism. The message acknowledges the authority Jesus has expressed in his teaching that has so astounded the crowds. The word from the cloud is the culminating moment of this visionary experience, vindicating Jesus by providing a foretaste of his glory. It is the imperative message of Mark's Gospel to his readers through the ages: "This is my Son, the Beloved; listen to him!" All our religious experiences convey this message, the light of our spiritual lives.

And then it's all over. Suddenly, there are just the four men on the mountain. They come down from the mountain, back into the flow of life. As the Gospel story continues, the disciples are very slow to understand the significance of what they have witnessed. Their experience does not, in itself, make them fully informed, brilliant, heroic, or holy. It is one experience on a long journey toward faithfulness.

Just as it would have been their mistake to preserve their experience, it would be our mistake to envy them theirs. Although there is some commonality to spiritual experience, there are differences that accommodate the differences between human beings. What was right for Elijah, or Moses, or the three disciples might be devastating to others. It is tempting to envy Paul his vision of the resurrected Lord, but even Paul was blinded for several days. Each of us has the experiences that are right for us. God's touch may be so gentle that we are scarcely aware or it; yet it may be all that we can bear. Whether suddenly or gradually, subtly or dramatically, the revelation of God has its effect.

Years later in a letter attributed to Peter, the transfiguration is recalled with an admonition we all can heed: "You will do well to be attentive to this [revelation of Jesus Christ] as to a lamp shining in a dark place, until the day dawns and the morning star rises in your hearts" (2 Peter 1:19b).

Nancy A. Willis is Assistant to the Rector
at Christ Church, Westerly, Rhode Island.

■ 2

PROCLAIMING IN LENT, HOLY WEEK, AND EASTER

ASH WEDNESDAY

Self-Examination and Saving Grace
Isaiah 58:1–12; Matthew 6:1–6, 16–21
Allyn Benedict

IN A FEW minutes we're all going to be invited, in the name of the church of God, to observe a holy Lent. As a part of that invitation, we will be reminded of what a holy Lent involves for us.

First, it would seem that we are going to be spending some time examining ourselves and repenting. You'll notice that the two are grouped together: self-examination and repentance. One follows the other. They are not listed as separate activities. There seems to be the assumption that if we have a really good look at ourselves, then we are going to discover some excellent reasons to repent.

There's a problem with this "self-examination" business though. It's a little like the United States Congress deciding to look into its own corruption. It's wise not to put much stock in the results. The questions they ask of themselves tend to be the kind that leads to safe and easy answers.

We, of course, are no different. We need help in asking the right questions. We need some guidelines to follow—a standard by which to measure ourselves that will put us in touch with truths that are neither safe nor easy.

The prayer book has something to say about this. The Litany of Penitence that we are going to say together soon presents us with a horrifying list of offenses of which it assumes we are guilty. You'll notice that there are no directions indicating that, if we think we're innocent of any particular sin, we can just sit that one out and listen. This list is convicting precisely because each and every offense is something of which each and every one of us is guilty.

Now, in spite of what the prayer book assumes, you may find yourself wanting to protest that you are innocent of some of these sins. If that's the case, and you're feeling particularly brave, I invite you to begin to pray: ask God to reveal to you the ways in which you personally live out that particular sin in your life. But this comes with a warning: don't ask if you don't want to know.

If we begin to measure ourselves by the measure found in the Litany of Penitence (and there's nothing in there that is not in line with the truth of God's Word), and as we begin to take seriously the fact that these things are what

18

God justly expects of us (otherwise we wouldn't have to turn in repentance when we fall short of them), then we begin to come up against the most difficult truth we have to face as Christians. We know the person we are supposed to be, but we also know that we are not that person.

We know what we are supposed to do, but we can't do it; we know what we're not supposed to do but we find ourselves doing those same things again and again. We just can't seem to make ourselves into the persons that we know God wants us to be. We've tried. It's not working out.

Not that our Savior hasn't done some wonderful work in us. But let's just say that his work isn't finished yet. We can see some results of Jesus' loving touch in our lives, but we still have not become persons who love God with our whole hearts. Forgiveness has won some measure of victory in our lives, but we still have trouble forgiving our enemies. Sometimes we fail miserably just trying to forgive our friends. Because most of us have begun to experience the love of our Savior and a measure of the freedom he promises, we want to know more about the person he calls us to be. We study his Word, we receive all kinds of teaching, and we become more and more aware of the radical nature of that call to follow him and of the difficulties of walking in new life.

It gets frustrating at times. He offers unconditional love, but he also calls us to face difficult truths. He pours out his love without measure, and does everything necessary to bring us new life; but he's not going to change his mind about the kind of life he wants to bring us, or about what it will cost us to have it.

Jesus insists that it's going to cost us our lives to have his life, and he doesn't seem to have an alternative plan. He never seems to say, "Well, my poor child, I can see that this is just too hard for you, so let's forget the whole thing. I'll just fix you all up without any further effort on your part." He's not going to save us without us. There's no cheap grace.

We can roll around on the floor and have a fit protesting that we're only human, and it's not fair when God expects us to do something we can't do, and God is always talking in riddles, and, after all, we didn't ask to be born. God never seems very impressed with that ploy.

The Lord wasn't impressed with Isaiah's people either. They were fed up and angry with him. Listen to what they say: "Why have we fasted, and thou seest it not? Why have we humbled ourselves, and thou takest no knowledge of it?"[1] In other words: "What have we been fasting for if you're not going to pay attention? We've been so humble it's sickening, and you don't seem to care one bit!"

These people want to do something, anything, to attract attention—to get on God's good side so that he'll give them what they want. Is this sounding at all familiar?

Isaiah's people may have figured—like one of today's pop singers—that God was watching them from a distance. So they grovel around on the ground in grain sacks, and they look up to see if he's noticing yet, and they dump ashes on their heads and look up again. "Is this humble enough? Aren't you impressed yet? Just look at me . . . I am pathetic; am I worthy of your pity, or what?"

The people Jesus is talking about in today's Gospel have gone even lower: They've given up trying to get God's attention. They're going to settle for something far less. Jesus says that they're doing all these pious acts in order to be seen by men. Well, men are easily impressed. (But I'll bet the women aren't buying it!)

Jesus knows what they're up to—they're giving their hearts away to the fickle praises of people. He knows what they need—to give their hearts to the only one who can bring them the light of truth. But they turn their faces away from the light by which they could see that the applause of other lost people is worth nothing.

The truth is that God not only sees their behavior, but God knows the secret rebellion of their hearts! The truth is that they are lost and in bondage.

So are we in every place where we turn from the source of our life. To face into that truth is to be very near the Kingdom of God. Because unless we know we are lost, and how we are lost, we will continue to give our hearts away to things that do not bring life.

Only those who know themselves to be lost begin to ask the questions for which Jesus is the answer. When that happens, Christian faith becomes a matter of life and death, and the foolish Gospel of Jesus Christ, crucified Lord and Savior, begins to look like the wisdom of God.

So the greatest gift that God can give us in this time of Lent is the gift of the truth about ourselves. We are sinners.

God's demands on us are just. We cannot appeal to the justice of God for our salvation.

Isaiah's people tried. They asked God for righteous judgments, and imagined that he was fooled by their outward show. God was watching them as they threw dirt on their heads. But God was not watching from a distance—he was watching from the inside. God knew the secrets of their hearts, and they were justly convicted.

So are we. But we have a Savior in Jesus Christ. The perfect answer to the justice of God. That answer is the love and mercy of God. Our Savior comes and finds us where we are, groveling one minute, strutting the next. Jesus brings us the truth, which is his life, freely given in love. As we confess the truth and receive his forgiveness we are enabled to forgive our enemies. Even to forgive ourselves.

As the love of Jesus grows in us, we become persons able to love others with the love he's given us. Because of the truth of who Jesus is, we can face the truth about who we are. We can be humble, not as a ploy to get on God's good side, but as the only response possible for people who know what it is to be loved and forgiven.

Those of us who receive ashes tonight are called to remember that, without the truth of our Savior, we will end as we began: as dust. But we put ashes on our head not to invoke God's pity. Since God's saving love has been poured out on us, we have no need for the false praise of people or for God's pity. If you receive ashes, they will be put on your forehead in the shape of a cross.

The words spoken will be these: "Remember that you are dust, and to dust you shall return." But the cross will remind us that those words are not God's last word.

That cross is the sign of our victory in Christ. Even as we stand in the truth of who we are, we are able to celebrate the Good News: We are not going to have the justice we think we want . . . . We are going to receive the mercy we need.

We are not going to get what we deserve. Death was what we deserved, but Jesus took that death on himself. And when God raised him from the dead, death was defeated. Because of that mighty act of love, something is possible that was not possible before. Instead of getting what we deserve, we're going to get what the Son of God deserves: eternal life with our Heavenly Father. This is the fulfillment of God's plan from the beginning. Jesus reaps what we sow and takes our sins on himself. In turn he invites us to reap what he has sown, and takes his resurrection life on us. What an exchange! What an offer! He's a wonderful Savior!

Allyn Benedict is Rector of Christ Church Parish, Watertown, Connecticut.

---

1. Isaiah 58:3a, RSV.

FIRST SUNDAY IN LENT

Talking to the Devil

Mark 1:9–13
Glenn E. Busch

I HAVEN'T talked with the devil lately. Well . . . actually, I guess it hasn't been all that long. You know how those things are. It seems as though you haven't been with someone for such a long time; but when you stop and think about it, you realize that you have had more contact than you remember.

As we begin another Lenten season, I decided, as part of my own study, to revisit the great Christian classic, *The Screwtape Letters*, by C. S. Lewis.[1] *The Screwtape Letters* are all about the devil, or the reality behind whatever word you choose to use for the existence of evil.

The book takes the form of letters from the devil, Screwtape, who sends his diabolical advice to his nephew, Wormwood, who has the assignment of negotiating a young man, known only as Patient, into the infernal regions. Screwtape gives Wormwood his devilish advice on how to capture the human heart. Behind the satire is a skillfully written book that gives uncanny insights into the human soul.

The first time I read *The Screwtape Letters*, many years ago, I was too green, too unsullied by the world to really appreciate it. It served more as entertainment then; but as I read it now, with more life experience behind me, and more regrets, I experience that uncomfortable wincing that occurs when you read something and notice yourself looking back at you from the pages. I commend it to you for Lenten reading. It is about, as the 1928 *Prayer Book* puts it, "the crafts and assaults of the devil."

Is this talk about the devil making you uncomfortable? Devil talk is blaze orange and we Episcopalians tend to prefer beige and banker blue. We don't talk about the devil very much. It is just not what we Episcopalians do. But I want you to know we meet the reality behind the devilish words right at the beginning of our Episcopal story. Described as a serpent in the narrative of creation, he remains an active part of our story right through to the end. Have you forgotten your baptism? Remember the promises: Do you renounce Satan and all the spiritual forces of wickedness that rebel against God? Do you renounce the evil powers of this world that corrupt and destroy the creatures of God? And remember our Gospel, one of the foundational stories of Lent, where Jesus himself was tempted by the devil. It is a defining moment in our Lord's life, occurring immediately after his baptism. Jesus meets Satan early on, and will encounter the forces of evil throughout his ministry, especially during the last hours of his life.

A good friend and colleague of mine, a highly respected and very talented priest of our church, had to take a leave of absence to enter a treatment program for the disease of alcoholism. He is now back at his duties and doing fine. I talked with him a couple of months ago, and as he was telling me his story, I could not help but think of the evil powers of this world that corrupt and destroy the creatures of God.

The part of the conversation that I remember most is when he was telling me about the baffling progress of his disease. "The fact is," he said, "I was fifty years old before I became drunk for the first time. Until that time, all through college, all those years as a rector of one of the biggest churches in the country, I only drank socially—wine with a meal, a social cocktail, that sort of thing—but I never got drunk until I was fifty. Then, it was like coming over the crest of a hill, a rapid downhill acceleration, until I was totally out of control. The disease just waited," he told me, "to manifest itself when I was most vulnerable to its seductive powers." Whatever the devil is, whatever that word represents, it is certainly patient and persistent. Satan is baffling, powerful, and cunning. In fact, often we don't even know that it is the devil to whom we are speaking. And that reminds me of my own last conversation with the Prince of Darkness.

Because our parish is very much a downtown church, we have all of the problems that accompany that distinction: trash and bottles in the yard, the need for a security system, and lots of people who come by asking for assistance—usually meaning "Give me some money." They come with all sorts of stories, a variety of attitudes, and many moods. I have been cajoled, cursed, threatened, sweet-talked, conned, and hustled. Sometimes, it gets on my nerves and corrupts my compassion.

A few months ago there was this woman. She seemed different from many of the others. She came one Sunday morning, a favorite time for the more experienced hustlers I know. A good time to catch the clergy when we are busy, and there are a lot of people around, and we might cough up twenty or twenty-five dollars in a hurry just to deal with the situation without asking many questions. But this lady seemed so sweet.

"May I help you?" I asked. "Yes," she said. "I am out of money and need diapers and formula for my baby." "Where do you usually get diapers and formula?" I asked. She hesitated—which should have made me suspicious—but then replied, "Rite Aid." "Okay," I said. "I'll write a check to Rite Aid, designated for diapers and formula, and you can go down there and get what you need."

A couple of weeks later my check came back. I noticed right away what she had done. Taking a broad-point pen she had written over my thin-line writing; and where it had said Rite Aid, she had written in her own name—or some name—and cashed it at an out-of-town convenience store. I can guarantee you it wasn't to buy diapers or formula. I was furious.

While it was a small matter—not much money was involved, and it certainly wasn't worth the trouble of pursuing—I was sick of this sort of abuse happening time and time again. I was tired of being lied to and scammed, tired of throwing away good money. I was tempted—really tempted—to see her in every needy person who comes through these doors. I was tempted to nurse my righteous indignation over the man who cursed me so vilely in front of my wife for not granting his monetary request. I was tempted to let these personal slights become an excuse for turning my back on all of the needy ones who come here.

I am starting to recall now the conversation I had with the devil on this matter, and I am beginning to remember his advice. I mean, don't we all just get fed up with those kinds of people ripping us off and stealing from us? Don't we have a right to just toss them out the door? To wash our hands of them? The devil really is a clever fellow. We often don't recognize his well-reasoned advice, nor that we are being tempted by the spiritual forces of wickedness that rebel against God. We expect the Prince of Darkness to be sinister, when actually he is the grand force of subtlety, very reasonable, charming, and convincing. We are also likely to think that the evil one's greatest temptations are the sensational ones, such as sex, money, booze, and gambling—the fluorescent temptations. That is not true either. That is just another deception in his bag of tricks. That is not where the real work of perdition gets done.

The work of hell is accomplished in the little things, in the mundane, day-to-day, small decisions that change minds and attitudes and points of view, and afflict the human heart. The real work of the devil is accomplished in the small resentment we hang onto. In that little grudge we just don't want to give up. It is accomplished in the raised eyebrow, in the snort of contempt. It is in the relative we refuse to forgive, in the self-righteous tone that we inflict on those who differ from us. It is in our refusal to get over hurt feelings, in the small uncharitable thoughts toward our neighbors and our colleagues. It is in the hatred that we think we disguise behind a well-mannered look, and it is present in our most imperceptible acts of hypocrisy. It is in our blindness to human need and suffering—that is where the real devil's work is done, in the common activities of our daily lives, each unsuspecting day, one day at a time.

At our last vestry meeting we had the most marvelous financial report that we have had in the history of our parish. Those of us who have been around here for a while were dumbfounded. Could our situation actually be that good? We had such a sensational stewardship effort and more pledges are still coming in. We have no debt, no bills to pay, and money in the bank. Many of us sat there thinking about where we have been, and how a few years ago we wouldn't have believed that we would be where we are today. It would be tempting, wouldn't it, after all the struggles and hard work, to coast for a while. We have earned it, we might think. And we might be tempted to sit back and take it easy and rest a bit: not to stretch ourselves to build another Habitat house, to move ahead with our ministry of outreach, to continually expand our programs. It sure would be tempting.

It is a good thing that Lent comes around each year. It helps us to remember the dark Spirit that is still present and eager to tempt us. I was thinking about that as I was leaving the church last week after the last Ash Wednesday service. I thought about it as we were singing the closing hymn, particularly the second verse. Perhaps you recall the words: "As thou with Satan didst contend and didst the victory win, O give us strength in Thee to fight, in Thee to conquer sin."

Yes, it is good that we have Lent. It is a special time to stop and think about the reality of evil. But I want you to remember that the devil tends to lie pretty low during this time of the year. With all of the piety and Lenten disciplines, and our focus on God's victory over sin, we tend to be on our best behavior during Lent. This isn't the devil's best time. But I want you to rest assured that he will be back. Just as soon as we have forgotten what Lent is all about, he'll be back—at a more opportune time.

Glenn E. Busch is Rector of St. Mary's Church, High Point, North Carolina.

---

1. C. S. Lewis, *The Screwtape Letters*, Revised Edition (New York: Collier Books, 1982).

THIRD SUNDAY IN LENT

Who Owns the Church?

Romans 7:13–25; John 2:13–22
Mike Kinman

And making a whip of cords, he drove them all, with the sheep and oxen, out of the temple; and he poured out the coins of the money-changers and overturned their tables. And he told those who sold the pigeons, "Take these things away; you shall not make my Father's house a house of trade!"

I imagine that I am in the minority of people who finds this passage among the most comforting in the gospels. On first glance, it certainly doesn't seem that comforting. It seems threatening. It seems threatening because it is filled with anger. And if there is one thing that often makes us decidedly uncomfortable, it's confronting anger. Confronting other people's anger. Confronting our own.

And yet here it is. Jesus is in the temple, and he isn't making small talk at coffee hour. He is angry. No doubt about it. And he's not just angry—he's that kind of angry when someone you deeply care about is really screwing up. I'm sure parents and children know this anger well.

Well, Jesus is so angry he makes a whip and starts whirling it in the air. He is so angry he starts overturning tables and pouring out containers. It's not our typical picture of Jesus. It makes Jesus seem a lot more like us than we usually consider. That can be difficult. But I think it can also be amazingly comforting.

I think an angry Jesus has a lot to offer us. If Jesus bridges the gap between God and us, I don't think that works unless he can get angry. Because anger is a part of being human. We all feel it. I have a lot of trouble relating to a Christ who never gets exasperated or frustrated or, not even every once in a while, gets truly furious at something. So I look at a Jesus who turns over a few tables, and I think maybe a Jesus who can get this upset is a Jesus who understands what it's like to be angry. Maybe a Jesus who can get this mad is a Jesus around whom I don't have to feel ashamed about my anger. Maybe this is a Jesus who understands anger and can help me work through it. Maybe this is a Jesus who understands me.

To me, that's comforting. But that's not all. Jesus' anger shows us that he is, indeed, human; but we also know that he is much, much more. So it is important not just to leave it at this, but to take a close look at exactly what evoked Jesus' anger. Jesus' frustration, Jesus' passion was directed against people to whom religion had become a business. More precisely, the temple had become about the people's business rather than God's. It had become an arena where the cares and concerns of their life—in this case, financial—were being acted out—not the will of God.

This begs two questions. The first is easier than the second: What is the church? As John plainly tells us, the church is not the building; the church is literally the body of Christ. His body. And as we Christians know so well, the body of Christ is *we*—bound together by baptism and sustained by the Eucharist. What is the church? The church is us.

Second question: Who owns the church? That becomes a much tougher question when you rephrase it in the terms of the first question. If we are the church, the question becomes not *who owns the church*, but *who owns us*, and that's tougher. None of us like to think that we are owned by anyone. It goes against our own feeling of what's right. It seems un-American, and perhaps therefore it seems to us un-Christian.

But the truth is, God *does* own us. We are God's own children. And as the body of Christ, we are God's church. We are, in Jesus' words, "my father's house." And really, thank God we are! Because the choice isn't *to be owned by God* or *not to be owned*. The choice, as Paul says in this morning's Epistle, is being owned by God or being slaves to our own sin. Because without God, that is what is left—our own sin and brokenness.

The truth is, if we are not owned by God—if we make our lives and the life of the church about our business instead of about God—we are doomed to sin and failure. Because without God, that's all there is.

Jesus turned over the tables in the temple, but he was doing more than that. Jesus turned upside down an entire notion of what the church is. The church is not something that exists for personal agendas and profit. The church is not here to make us feel good. The church is not here for individual betterment. The church is not even here so we can do good works.

The church is here for the glory of God. Period. Nothing less. And there can be nothing more. And who is the church? The church is us. So let's put it in those terms and see how that sounds.

We do not exist for our own personal agendas and profit. We are not here to make ourselves feel good. We are not here for our own individual betterment. We are not even here to do good works. We are here for the glory of God. Period. Nothing less. And there can be nothing more.

It's an uncomfortable notion at first, every bit as uncomfortable as the Good Shepherd cracking the whip. But really, it is the most comfortable reality there is. Because when we recognize that we are here for the glory of God and not for ourselves, that is when we find our salvation. That is when we turn the corner from jumping between one thing and another, trying to fill the holes that gape inside us. We turn the corner to a joy that can never be greater—the joy of life in Christ. A life where we don't just call Jesus Lord, but where we live it. If that life is at our center, we cannot fail.

It is ironic, isn't it? The only way we can actually accomplish what we all most deeply want—our own ultimate happiness—is to forsake the quest for it. To forsake our own agendas and to give ourselves over to God. To recognize that we are God's house. We are God's people. Otherwise, we will in our blindness keep on doing precisely what is worst for us and the church will become more and more of an empty shell.

So what does that mean for us? What does that mean for this parish, the Episcopal Church of St. Michael and St. George? Well, what it means is that this entire place—all its beauty, its splendor, its life, all the beautiful vestments and exquisite music and incredible outreach programs and exciting new youth ventures, all of the amazing pastoral care we give to one another, all the times we support each other in time of need, all the remarkable insights we receive when we study Scripture together, all the pain and all the promise, all the life and all the death, everything this great place has been, is, and will be, past, present, and future—all of it means absolutely nothing if we are not of God.

If we are not the Father's house, if we are not about living for the glory of God, then each one of these wonderful things is at best a harmless diversion to pass the time until we die, and at worst a dangerous distraction that builds up a false sense of our own righteousness apart from God. A distraction that only serves to separate us even further from the Creator, who loves us, yearns for us, and is patiently waiting for us to come home.

Jesus was passionate about this—so passionate that he displayed a burst of anger that most of us only dream about. He was passionate because he loves us without bounds, and this is the hinge upon which our entire life rests. And because he loves us so much, he doesn't back down—he passionately throws the challenge right in our faces—into yours, into mine, into all of ours. A challenge that is not to be answered with pointing fingers and assigning of blame, but with every last one of us searching our own hearts and supporting others as they do the same.

The challenge he gives us is simple: Are we about God or are we about ourselves? Whose business is being transacted in this house? And if, when we search our souls, the answer is anything but "my Father's business," if our agenda is anything but the glory of God, then something has gone very, very wrong.

But think about this. Every time we search our souls and answer "my Father's business," every time we let go of our own personal agendas and desires and truly be the church of God—the body of Christ—we can and should rejoice. Rejoice because we are a part of the most remarkable ongoing event in human history—the coming of the Kingdom of God. Rejoice because we are part of the transforming of the world into the image of Christ, for the glory of God. Rejoice because we are part of a building up instead of a tearing down. Rejoice because we are a people called, not just a people assembled.

We can rejoice, because when we let God be our center, we are not just a people doing, but a people being. Being Christ to each other. Living, loving, saving, caring, sometimes singing, sometimes dancing, sometimes crying, sometimes being so mad that it's all we can do to leave the tables right side up. Are we human? You bet. Will we stumble and trip? Absolutely. But as long as we are about God's business, as long as we work for God's glory, we cannot fail.

That is our challenge. That is our comfort. That is our salvation.

Mike Kinman is Associate Rector for Youth and Young Adult Ministry at the Church of St. Michael and St. George, St. Louis, Missouri.

FOURTH SUNDAY IN LENT

Fragments of Our Lives

John 6:4–15
C. Denise Yarbrough

Gather up the fragments left over, so that nothing may be lost.

This has been one of those weeks when reading the newspaper has caused me to gasp and to rage at the forces of nature and life that bring so much anguish to so many. There were floods in the Midwest that caused at least twenty deaths and much property destruction. There were tornadoes in Arkansas, leaving homes and businesses in rubble. And on Friday, there were horrific pictures of a church school van, flattened and shredded by a tree blown over in Thursday's gale-force winds. That accident killed four little girls on their way to school in Queens. As I looked at the pictures of those four little girls, all about my own daughter's age, and read of the anguish and grief of their parents and friends, my mother's heart broke for those parents. I watch my own children board a school bus every morning. Never would I expect not to hear them crash through the door in the afternoon, calling out to me, then rushing off to play with their friends.

As I looked at pictures of homes destroyed by flood and tornadoes, I was once again caught up short with how incredibly fragile our lives really are, and how quickly everything can change. All of us here have been reeling from the shock of the auto accident that has put Jennifer Brown in the hospital, an event that has brought home to our own faith community the fragility of all our lives. All of these events remind us starkly that one minute there is apparent wholeness, the next minute total fragmentation. Lives once carefully constructed and put together are suddenly fragmented and torn asunder. How, I asked myself, is God present in the midst of these fragments?

Today's Gospel story of the feeding of the five thousand is well known to all of us. It appears in all four Gospels in some variation or another. The version we hear today, from John's Gospel, contains a couple of interesting variations on the story that do not appear in the other accounts. In John's story, a little boy provides the two fishes and five barley loaves, which are then blessed and broken by Jesus to feed the crowd. It is neither Jesus nor the disciples who provide the food that ultimately nourishes so many, but a little one in the needy crowd. And only in John's Gospel does Jesus say to his disciples, after the crowd has finished eating, "Gather up the fragments left over, so that nothing may be lost." They do as he says and the result is twelve baskets of fragments, leftovers, scraps—more nourishment than was originally provided by the little boy.

"Gather up the fragments left over, so that nothing may be lost." Why is Jesus so concerned with gathering up the fragments? Of what use are the fragments, anyway? Aren't fragments of the feast the expendable bits, the stuff to be thrown away, that which is useless, unwanted, and preferably forgotten? But there is profound truth embedded in that little sentence. When we gather up the fragments of our lives and allow nothing to be lost, we may find we have more than we started with, not less. Perhaps the breaking and fragmenting that happens to all of us on life's journey is the way we are being used by God as those loaves were used. Perhaps the end result is abundance and surplus, not scarcity and want.

What better time than Lent to contemplate the fragments of our lives? Initially, it seems peculiar that our lectionary would inject, in the middle of Lent—a season of fasting, penitence, and self-examination—a story about feeding and about God's capacity to yield abundance in the face of apparent paucity. An amazing miracle story, a glimmer of hopefulness in the midst of the somber Lenten season.

On Ash Wednesday, our liturgy invited us to observe "a Holy Lent, by self-examination and repentance; by prayer, fasting and self-denial; and by reading and meditating on God's Holy Word." Traditionally, Lent has been a time for reflection, for self-examination, for looking at the dark and dusty places in our lives, and offering those to God. Perhaps Lent is a peculiarly appropriate time to consider the fragments of our lives and to gather those fragments together "so that nothing may be lost."

How important "fragments" are in many different arenas of human life! A psychologist or psychiatrist will often tell a client that even a fragment of a dream may contain a clue to important unconscious processes going on in the psyche. Archeologists can piece together substantial information about ancient cultures and lifestyles from fragments of papyri, or pots, or implements and tools used by an ancient culture. Detectives often solve criminal cases based on little fragments of evidence: a piece of clothing, a lock of hair, a footprint.

When I was a little girl I loved to rummage in my grandmother's attic—she was a pack rat of the first order—where I found pieces and fragments of her life and of my great-grandparents' lives in diaries, letters, photographs, bits of clothing, pieces of jewelry, and in old, broken toys. Fragments—the little broken pieces—often carry with them tremendous significance and important information. Indeed, they are often imbued with the very essence of the person to whom they belonged. And some of them are treasured memories, cherished objects that are kept locked in safe places to keep happy memories alive, while other fragments in our lives are pieces broken off when something shatters us and tears our life in pieces. Those fragments are the ones we most often want to throw away, to put the pain behind us and move on. Yet Jesus says, "Gather up the fragments left over, so that nothing may be lost." He seems to call us to gather all the fragments, not just the pleasant ones.

Most of us, I wager, would prefer to lose some of the fragments of our lives, if possible. Those places where we feel most broken—unrealized dreams, dashed hopes, failures, wearying struggles (that are sometimes overwhelming), the loss of a child, parent, or spouse, illness, natural disaster, divorce, job loss, trouble with children or family, aging parents and grandparents (with all the responsibilities attendant to their needs), conflicting roles that leave us feeling fragmented internally. All these bits and pieces of life that break each of us in some way or another are fragments we'd like to lose. We are tempted to kick away the painful fragments as quickly as possible and get on with life. Indeed, we often have to do so just to keep going. But Jesus calls us to "gather up the fragments left over, so that nothing may be lost." Perhaps our personal and collective fragments are actually crucial pieces of who we are and are to be treasured and kept, rather than forgotten.

Gathering the fragments of our lives is sometimes painful. Looking at those dusty places, examining the broken pieces—dreams not realized, hopes dashed, love lost, failures and setbacks, feelings of inadequacy or shame or guilt, parts of ourselves that we wish weren't there, that we didn't have to remember—seem to be called forth in this fragment-gathering exercise.

I grew up under a priest who was a firm believer in the sacrament of confession and who encouraged me to make a private confession as part of my Lenten discipline. In all my years in his church I never did so—fearing the self-examination required to do such a thing and not wanting to expose all those fragments of myself to God, never mind a human priest. I was thirty-six years old before I could examine all those fragments and offer them to God in the sacrament of confession. And I was able to do so only after I had experienced—and knew in the depth of my being—God's love and acceptance of all of me—fragmented though that "me" may be. Confession is a way of gathering up the fragments—reviewing, remembering, and letting go—and giving them back to God. It is the religious equivalent of therapy, and both seem to me to be a gathering up of the fragments, so that nothing is lost.

In the story we heard today, the fragments amounted to twelve baskets after they had been gathered up. There is clearly a message of abundance and prosperity in this image of the twelve baskets of leftovers. And one suggesting that this fragment-gathering endeavor is not a solitary one, but a communal effort. The twelve baskets the disciples collected represented the fragments of the activity of thousands of people. Perhaps any one person's crumbs would have been minuscule and not worth collecting; but together the fragments amounted to something substantial.

As a Christian community we must consider the importance of gathering our collective fragments together. We do not *act* alone, and we are not called to *be* alone, even in our fragmentation and brokenness. We all come together in this community to worship God, to serve Christ, and to be a community of love, bringing to this community our own peculiar fragments, combining those with the fragments of others to produce an overflowing basket of nourishment for a starving world.

Certainly in Lent we appropriately focus on the ultimate symbol of fragmentation—Jesus on the cross—as we prepare to relive his passion and death and to celebrate his resurrection. Ours is a faith in which fragmentation and redemption are connected—when we celebrate the Eucharist, we share in the broken body of Christ while remembering, celebrating, and participating in Christ's resurrection and continuing presence in our lives and our world. In the cross, we see starkly before our eyes a God who suffers with us and shares our brokenness and fragmentation. God entered human history and suffered and died on a cross to transform the future of human history from a future bound for destruction and death to one moving toward abundant, eternal life.

Our participation in the process of gathering up the fragments so that nothing may be lost is required, so that all of us, living, loving, and working together as a community of fragments, can collectively amount to a heaping basket of abundance. None of us can do this alone. We come to the altar rail each week, offering "ourselves, our souls and bodies" to God and to each other, to partake in the body and blood of Christ who was broken for us, forming a community of fragments that together amounts to a basket of abundance.

Neither God nor we are able to prevent the fragmenting experiences from happening. Indeed they are an essential part of our journey. As the little boy supplied the two fishes and five loaves, so we supply ourselves, our lives, our love to each other and to God. And when we are broken by the inevitable struggles and tragedies of life, God will bless that brokenness, and our individual fragments will be gathered together with the fragments of the rest of the human family to yield a teeming basket of God's abundant love.

C. Denise Yarbrough is Assistant Rector at Trinity Church, Toledo, Ohio.

Palm Sunday

Standing Naked—Given New Clothes

Mark 14:32–15:47
Michael B. Ferguson

THE YOUNG MAN sat with his back against the olive tree. He was part of the group who often came to quiet places with Jesus, to pray and to listen for God's response. On this tension-filled night, Jesus left most of them near the entrance to the garden, while he, Peter, James, and John went a little farther up the path.

At first the young man had been disappointed that he was not included in the small group Jesus gathered close around him. As he sat under the tree, letting his mind and heart open up to God, he reviewed the momentous events of the past three years. He had left home at seventeen to follow Jesus. Jesus' preaching had moved him to tear himself away from his family to follow this gentle man who taught a radically new approach to performing essential Jewish ministry. One can't do God's work bound up in legalisms. It was simple, Jesus said. Show your love for God by caring for your neighbor. By providing food and clothing and shelter. By inviting even the scruffiest beggar to share your meager meal.

The young man had followed Jesus all over Galilee and Judea. He had watched Jesus heal lepers and people with other diseases. He had been part of the group who distributed bread and fish to thousands of hungry people who came to hear Jesus teach—people who had been touched by Jesus' message that God loved them all.

Earlier this week the young man had been part of Jesus' entourage as he entered Jerusalem. Like so many others, the young man got caught up in the fervor of the procession and joined in the shouts of "Hosanna! Blessed is the One who comes in the name of the Lord!" He followed Jesus to the temple and helped him drive out those who were perverting God's house with their idolatry of money and power. He had moved close to Jesus as the tension mounted. He sensed an ugliness that told him that something bad would soon happen to this man who had touched him deeply. He had vowed to protect Jesus at all costs, even giving up his own life if necessary.

Now, as he listens for God's response, his worst fears are realized. With blinding speed Judas brings a crowd into the garden. As the young man starts to step between Jesus and a man brandishing a club, the man attacks him. His nerve fails and he turns to run. The man grabs his tunic, but the young man shrugs it off and runs away naked. As he flees, he hears laughter and taunts from the crowd. "Let him go," someone yells. "He won't be any danger without clothes. He'll be easy to find when we need him. He can't hide that way."

In many ways we are that young man. Our hearts have been touched by Jesus. We have been taught to pray by Jesus. Jesus has given us ministry to do, and we have tried to do it faithfully. Jesus has let us assist while he healed someone. Jesus has healed us in one way or another; perhaps many.

We have followed Jesus into Jerusalem, waving palm branches and shouting, "Hosanna!" We have wondered why Jesus didn't include us in his very inner circle, saying to ourselves that we would be more faithful than someone else, that we wouldn't fall asleep after Jesus asked us to stay alert. We have assured ourselves that we would give our lives to protect Jesus. We have turned and fled from Jesus' side when someone larger or louder has threatened us, shrugging off our cloak of Christianity.

Standing there without clothes is not a comforting feeling. We know we can't hide when we're naked, so we go looking for clothes. Too often the clothes we find are those of someone who doesn't believe in Jesus. We *can* hide that way, we think. Hide behind laughter at jokes made at the expense of people who are different than we are. Hide by turning our backs on a sister or brother in need. Hide by saying, "I won't go to church this week, so my friends won't think I can't take care of myself."

Jesus may have been disappointed when the young man fled into the night, stumbling naked down the path and out of the garden. Disappointed, but not surprised. Jesus must be disappointed when we do the same thing. Disappointed, but not surprised.

But Jesus found an important ministry for the young man. Many believe he's the same young man who speaks to Mary Magdalene and the other women, telling them that Jesus has been raised. The young man represents all who have been baptized into Jesus' resurrection. He is given new clothes and a new ministry. Jesus does the same for us. Even though we turn and run, stumbling naked down the path and out of the garden, Jesus calls and empowers us to tell all who come into our lives, seeking to see Jesus, that he has indeed been raised and goes before us into the Galilees of our lives.

Michael B. Ferguson is Rector of St. Anne's Church, Appomattox, Virginia.

GOOD FRIDAY

Behold Your Family

John 19:25–27
Valerie B. Carnes

". . . Behold, your son! . . . Behold, your mother!"

IT WAS JUST two years ago today that Ronnie died.

No reason why you should know that. You didn't know Ronnie. Neither did I, except for the last few hours of his life.

Ronnie was an eleven-year-old African-American boy who was shot on the way to a Good Friday service in his neighborhood church on Chicago's South side.

Ronnie's neighborhood was full of gangs, and one of those gangs chose Good Friday afternoon of 1995 for a shootout—something to do with gang turf and drugs. Ronnie never had anything to do with the gangs. He just happened to be in the wrong place at the wrong time.

Ronnie was brought to the Northwestern Memorial Hospital emergency room, where I was a student chaplain. Within the hour his family had gathered around him—his mother, his grandmother, his two sisters, and his cousin Sam. There were also several nurses and Ellen, a pediatric specialist, along with Sister Katherine, the other chaplain, and me.

Ronnie died just before midnight, in the final hours of Good Friday. Just after he died, his nine-year-old cousin, Sam, stood up, squared his shoulders, and knelt down by Ronnie's mother.

"Don't cry, Aunt Tish," he whispered, taking her hand. "I promised Ronnie I'd always take care of you if anything happened to him around the neighborhood. I won't let you down. It's all up to me now."

The other chaplain that night, Sister Katherine, was a Dominican sister who saw Scriptural parallels in every situation. She looked around at the scene by Ronnie's bed and whispered: "Just look at us! Here we are, sitting at the foot of the cross. We're even hearing 'Woman, behold your son' and 'Son, behold your mother.' Oh, this is Good Friday, all right."

It was Good Friday then, that rainy day two years ago, and it is again today. The friends of Jesus, huddled at the foot of the cross, were like Ronnie's family. They knew that they would be the survivors, the ones left behind. It would be up to them, just as Sam said—up to them to carry on without Jesus, their rabbi and leader and friend.

"Up to them" means it's up to us. For Jesus set in motion a whole new network of relationships, a new community when he spoke these words from the cross. Jesus, hanging alone on the cross, saw below him two of the people in his life who were most important—the two who were most bound to him in love, who were faithful to him through the long hours of his dying.

As Jesus spoke to them, he redefined their understanding of family. And ours. Woman, this is your son. Friend, this is now your mother. This is your new family by adoption.

In this poignant moment Jesus gives us a new understanding of family. "Family" becomes more than genetic accident, more than our family of origin.

"Family" in God's new order of things is inclusive, reaching out to embrace our soul siblings and spiritual parents, those who are faithful to us even when we are least faithful to them. It includes both those whom we know and those we've never even met.

In this Gospel, Jesus models for us what we are all called to do: to care for one another, to "adopt" one another as God has graciously adopted us.

Some theologians see this poignant moment as the beginning of church, the first time in Scripture that a community of care and concern is named and instituted, with Mary as its mother and the beloved disciple as its new leader. And that takes us back to the story where we began.

After Ronnie's death, the young boy's family and friends grew into a community-action group that joined forces with the neighborhood churches and with Sister Katherine's religious order.

A year after Ronnie's death, the gangs had moved out. The people had taken back their neighborhood and reclaimed its streets and alleys. There was new life everywhere—fresh paint on the houses, gardens planted in vacant lots, new awnings and storefronts. What had seemed the end for Ronnie's family of origin brought new life to a dying neighborhood.

Ronnie's extended family was now the whole neighborhood—African-American, Asian-American, Caucasian-American—an inclusive new family that stood for rebirth and renewal, for life transformed by love of God and other people.

Today, on this Good Friday, Jesus speaks to us from the cross, reminding us that family goes beyond the accident of birth to include all persons as our brothers and sisters, parents and children.

Jesus calls us out of the narrowly insular and the parochial—the view that only our family, our parish, our class or race or ethnic group or gender or denomination is the "right" one; that only we count and no one else matters. Jesus calls us out of a narrow view of family to an affirming, inclusive, and all-embracing one.

A world of disparate cultures and experiences is drawn into unity through the person of Jesus: "Whoever does the will of God is my brother and sister and mother." From the cross, Jesus speaks the blessing of inclusive community to all of us, to you and me. Jesus calls us as he called Mary and John: Behold. Rise above your grief for me and look around you.

So let's do that. I invite you to look around you, right now. Look around you and behold. Behold the person next to you, in front of you, behind you. Look at that person and behold your brother, your sister, your parent or child in Christ.

Behold our brother, our Savior, Jesus the Christ, Son of the living God.

So: welcome home. Welcome to the family, our new family in Christ.

Valerie B. Carnes is Chaplain to Alexian Village of Tennessee, and Priest Associate of Grace Church, Chattanooga, Tennessee.

EASTER DAY

An Easter Story for Adults

Mark 16:1–8
William J. Eakins

I WAS IN THE MALL a couple of weeks ago. The jacket of a book caught my eye in one of the bookstores. The book was entitled *The Easter Story for Children.* I was curious, and I opened it up. As I suspected, it was largely about bunnies, chicks, and flowers, with a little about Jesus thrown in at the end. But the book got me thinking. What, I wonder, would be *The Easter Story for Adults?* I suggest the Gospel reading that we have just heard this morning.

It is a story that begins in the pain, bewilderment, and anxiety that adults know is an all-too-real part of the human experience. Three women make their way out of the city at the first light of dawn to visit a tomb. They're sick with grief over the death of Jesus. Their minds ache with the gruesome memories of his recent crucifixion, and their hearts are heavy with the realization that not only will they not see their friend anymore, but all the hopes that Jesus had raised within them are now over. No more brave talk about the Kingdom of God's being at hand with God's justice and God's righteousness; nothing more to look forward to now but, at best, the continuation of the same old world with all of its oppression and injustice. Death and a foreboding sense of a dark future are all the women can think of as they make their way, appropriately enough, to the tomb.

Who among us has not felt at some time and in various ways like those three women? The doctor calls. "I'm sorry; it's malignant. We'll do the best we can." The phone rings in the night. "Sir, there's been an accident. Please come quickly." They sit down at the dinner table. "You know we really love you, honey, but Mommy and Daddy have decided that we can't be married to each other anymore." She walks into the office. "You have a month's severance pay. It has nothing to do with you; we're downsizing and have decided we must close your department." In our own ways that are all different but somehow all the same, we have all experienced crucifixion and death. The Easter story for adults, the real Easter story, begins not in a sunny spring meadow but in a death and in a tomb.

One of the stories told at the Nuremberg war trials was that of a group of Jews who had escaped from the gas chambers and taken refuge in a cemetery. They lived there, huddled and hidden in the pits that had been dug to serve as houses of death. One night, a baby was born in one of the graves. The gravedigger, an old Orthodox Jew, assisted at the birth. When the babe uttered his first cry, the gravedigger exclaimed, "Great God, have you finally sent the Messiah? For who but Messiah would be born in a grave?" Who, indeed, we Christians would echo, and, in a sense, it is our conviction as Christians that Messiah was indeed born in a grave. At least it is in a grave that our faith that Jesus is the Messiah, the Christ, is born. That is a faith that tells us nothing in life, no matter how painful and deadly, can separate us from God. It is a faith that nothing is over until God says it is over, and that God's love never ends.

The three women approach the rock-hewn cave that is Jesus' tomb, and they wonder who will roll away the round and heavy stone door. It is then that they are stunned to discover that the stone has already been rolled back. They enter the tomb and they find it empty. Jesus' body is nowhere to be seen. But there is an angelic messenger who tells them not to be alarmed: Jesus is not in the tomb because he has been raised from the dead. "But go, tell his disciples and Peter that he is going ahead of you to Galilee; there you will see him, just as he told you."[1]

Now if this were a story for children, we might expect that the two Marys and Salome, having seen the empty grave and having heard the message of Jesus' resurrection, would run out of the tomb laughing, smiling, and running to tell the Good News to others. To be sure, some of the other Gospel accounts of the resurrection tell of such a response. Mark, however, gives what I believe is the adult version of the Easter story. The three women, he tells us, "fled from the tomb" in "terror" and "amazement," and "they said nothing to anyone, for they were afraid."[2]

Now isn't that a thoroughly reasonable and realistic response to the Easter message? The authentic Easter story is, after all, not a little tale about nature—life emerging in the spring, butterflies bursting from the chrysalis, chicks pecking their way from eggs, tulips rising from the hard soil. The real, the adult, Easter story is about an impossibility, a miracle, God's raising Jesus from the dead. It is about Jesus' resurrection to new and wondrous life, not merely the survival of his Spirit or the enduring truth of his teaching. Furthermore, the real Easter, the adult Easter, is about a Jesus Christ who lives today, not just long ago—a living Lord who is always one step ahead of his disciples.

Perhaps we have heard the Easter story so many times that we have become casual about it. So we come to church this morning, sing the hymns, smell and admire the flowers, listen to the brass, and go away thinking: "What a lovely service! What a nice Easter!" If, however, we were to let ourselves catch a glimpse, even for a moment, of the true Easter, we would leave this church more like those three women fled the tomb, overcome by amazement and holy fear.

The real Easter story is not merely a charming tale: it is a proclamation that puts a claim upon us. If Jesus Christ rose from the dead, then maybe he is the Son of God, the Savior, and our rightful Lord. If so, then maybe we should, no *must*, do as he said, take up our cross and follow him. Perhaps this dying and following is also the way that leads to new life. But we'll never know unless we try it. The Easter story for adults invites us to be grown-ups who are willing to take the risky but rewarding adventure of being Jesus' disciples.

"Go and tell," the Easter angel says. That command is an important reminder that the Easter story for adults involves social responsibility as well as personal belief. The true Easter story, unlike counterfeits such as the Heaven's Gate cult, offers not an escapist fantasy but rather an engagement with the world of flesh and blood here and now. In this world, Christians are to bear witness to their faith in a risen Lord by how they live. The world will know that Christ lives because he lives in us.

Perhaps one of the reasons *The Easter Story for Children* is so popular even with adults is that we can hear it and walk away unchallenged and unchanged. *The Easter Story for Adults*, however, is very different. It begins where we are, in all our human brokenness, and offers us the promise of new life. It is a story that—if we hear and believe it—will never let us be the same again. Those who first heard it fled in fear and amazement and told no one because they were afraid. We know, however, that this was only their initial response. Soon those women, along with the other first Christians, came to believe that Christ was risen indeed; and they became a part of a mighty enterprise that turned the ancient world upside down.

If we hear and believe *The Easter Story for Adults*, we will do the same.

William J. Eakins is Rector of Trinity Church, Hartford, Connecticut.

---

1. Mark 16:7.
2. Mark 16:8.

SECOND SUNDAY IN EASTER

The Wounds of the Risen Christ

John 20:19–31
Catherine Woods Richardson

HOW DO WE recognize the risen Christ? In the Easter stories we hear this time of year, we know that Jesus' disciples and friends did not always recognize him at first. Mary Magdalene mistook Jesus for the gardener as she sat weeping outside the tomb. Two disciples walked and talked with Jesus for hours along the road to Emmaus on that first Easter Sunday, thinking him a stranger. In today's Gospel reading from John, the disciples are hiding in fear on the evening of Easter Day. Jesus appears among them, greets them in peace, then shows them his hands and his side. Thomas, who was not with them, does not believe that Christ has risen: "Unless I see in his hands the print of the nails, and place my finger in the mark of the nails, and place my hand in his side, I will not believe."[1] When Jesus appears again, he invites Thomas to do just this: to touch his wounded hands and side.

Now I do not know how Jesus looked when he rose from the dead. I expect we all have our own images, influenced by two millennia of Christian art. The risen Christ is often portrayed as a dazzling figure in white robes, surrounded by light. But the Gospels do not tell us much of Jesus' appearance, either before or after his death. But they do tell us one thing: when Jesus rose from the dead, he still bore the marks of his torture and death. And it was by these wounds that his disciples knew him.

Jesus' wounds are important. They tell us that the resurrection did not erase Jesus' suffering and death. When Jesus returns from the dead, it is not as if the crucifixion never happened. But the risen Jesus is also somehow new and different from the one who died, so different that his wounds become a point of identification. His wounds are the marks that prove to the disciples that he is indeed the same person they knew. Through the resurrection, Jesus has been transformed into something new, and yet he bears his old life in the scars that mark his hands and side and feet.

The wounds of the risen Christ are signs not only of what the resurrection meant for Jesus, but also of what the resurrection means for us. Jesus' resurrection does not wipe away suffering and death. The risen Christ still carries the knowledge of suffering and death in his body, and we still bear suffering and death in this world. The resurrection does not keep bad things from happening any more than it offers any explanation of why they do. The resurrection does not answer our question of "Why, God, does this happen?" In the face of violence, death, despair, and grief, Jesus' resurrection offers not an answer, but a promise.

And the promise is this: not that our sufferings will be erased but that they, and we, will be profoundly transformed. Pain and death, though real, are not the end. They do not define us. New life and joy await us; indeed, they are already here. We are redeemed. A God who knows our pain and the sufferings of this world makes us new. The risen Christ is no transcendent figure, rising above the sorrows of the world, but one marked forever by his life and death as a human being. It is through his wounds that he knows our pain, and it is through his wounds that he reaches out to us in love, healing, and reconciliation. By his wounds we are healed.

After Jesus invites Thomas to touch his hands and side, he says, "Have you believed because you have seen me? Blessed are those who have not seen and yet believe."[2] The word translated "blessed" in John's Gospel can also be read as "fortunate" or "happy." When Jesus says, "Blessed are those who have not seen and yet believe," he does not mean that the faithful will receive a special blessing from God, but that they already are blessed by virtue of their faith. Their faith is their blessing. Happy and fortunate indeed are those who do not need to see, who already believe, who do not wait for more proof, who do not face the torments of doubt and uncertainty. Happy are those who trust in God and in God's work of resurrection.

This past summer, I spent ten weeks in training as a hospital chaplain. And one of the things I discovered in ministering to sick and dying people is that with some people, it is awfully hard to tell who the minister really is. Now I'm not talking about those patients and hospital staff who looked out for me, and made sure I was comfortable, and asked me how I was doing—though I met many gracious people. I mean instead those individuals who had such a depth of faith and generosity of spirit that I had nothing to offer them. God's promise of comfort and hope already rested far deeper in their hearts and souls than it did in mine.

This past Friday, a friend who has also worked as a hospital chaplain told me a story of meeting a person like this. My friend told me that in the course of her work at a particular hospital, she met a small, elderly woman who suffered greatly from rheumatoid arthritis. The arthritis was so bad that her body was permanently bent, "curled up like a sowbug," my friend told me, and this woman could only lie on her side in the hospital bed. At their first meeting, my friend entered the hospital room, introduced herself as the chaplain and asked what she might do to be of help. And this small woman, curled up in a tight little ball on her bed, replied, "Well, I don't rightly know. I can't read or watch TV, and I really can't do much of anything at all, lying here all day, but maybe you could bring me a list of names of people who need prayers, so I can pray for them."

As chaplains, my friend and I have seen many responses to the pain and uncertainty hospital patients face, some more generous than others. But this woman's request to pray for total strangers was rare indeed. In this hospital room, my friend found a woman blessed in faith, a woman who in the midst of great pain already knew resurrection, a woman who believed. Happy and fortunate she was, even in her suffering, for her faith, and not her suffering, defined who she was and gave her strength to embrace the world in love.

Jesus told Thomas, "Blessed are those who have not seen and yet believe." And this is true. But it is also true that wherever we see a wounded, suffering person reaching out in love and generosity to a world still filled with pain, we see the risen Christ. This is how we recognize him.

We are surrounded with the signs of resurrection. Thanks be to God.

Catherine Woods Richardson is Rector of
Grace Church, Traverse City, Michigan.

1. John 20:25b, RSV.
2. John 20:29b, RSV.

SIXTH SUNDAY IN EASTER

A Message So Good As to Border on Folly

1 John 4:7–21
Stephen E. Carlsen

SEVERAL MONTHS ago, I received a new translation of *The Odyssey*. It so happened that I had just finished listening to a Books-on-Tape recording of *The Iliad*. What has stuck me over the years as I have read and listened to the Homeric epics is how much better, how much nobler, are the human heroes than the gods in these stories. The gods are vindictive, petty, and even lecherous. They are deceitful. They play favorites. They make a sport out of human affairs. Calypso keeps poor Odysseus prisoner on her island, far from his Ithaca, far from his wife and family, because the goddess wants him as her own. Poseidon, the earth shaker, the God of the seas, keeps Odysseus from making it home, because Odysseus blinded the Cyclops, his son. Athena, on the other hand, is Odysseus's champion. And on Olympus, the gods vie with each other, using poor Odysseus as a pawn in their power struggles.

No wonder Socrates discouraged exposing the youth of Athens to the poets because of the unethical examples of the gods contained in Greek poetry. He preferred to give the gods their due but to leave them alone, so much so that at his trial one of the charges against him was of atheism.

Nevertheless, this view of the gods, namely that they should be placated but left alone, was common throughout the ancient world. Offer the appropriate sacrifices. Violate no sacred places. Harm no priests. Do not draw attention to yourself so that the gods do not become too involved with you. Any glory won from the gods is offset by a greater measure of suffering.

On the face of it, this is not an unreasonable view of things. Given the fickle nature of glory and of fortune in this life, given our vulnerability to changes in our financial, physical, or romantic status, why would anyone think that the hidden causes operative behind all things, that is, the gods, are anything but fickle? Why should we view the gods as anything but capricious and erratic?

I daresay that many today still live their lives this way. We get a lot of people coming through here, for baptisms, confirmations, weddings, and funerals, who wish to "do the right thing," to offer the appropriate respect religiously, but who also keep a distance, avoiding too much exposure to the divine. For some reason, they think it important to get the imprint, perhaps the approval, of God at crucial moments in their lives or in the lives of their children, but they are wary of any greater exposure. They seem to be playing it safe, doing what is expected, following convention—but no more.

In what is now being called by many a post-Christian age, such pagan behavior is to be expected. After all, good, upright pagans have never been irreligious. They have accepted the God or gods offered them by their culture. They pay those gods their due respect—to get a blessing or to ward off harm. They just resist allowing any greater religious claim on their lives. Perhaps it is too much trouble. Perhaps they do not see why the gods deserve any greater worship. Perhaps they are afraid of the gods and wish not to draw attention to themselves by being either too religious or not religious enough. Perhaps, as is most likely, they do not see what the gods have to do with themselves.

I am of two minds about such people who approach us. Sometimes I feel like asking them why they bother. On the other hand, I think baptisms, weddings, and funerals are occasions when they can discover that the church is of value. That God is not distant and fickle, but near and present, constant. That God in Christ does have something to do with our lives, and that this relationship is not arbitrary but gentle, warm, and gracious.

Our Epistle for this Sunday contains the well-known verse: "God is love." We have become familiar with this idea, maybe too familiar. We do not realize what an astounding idea of God this is. To the ancient pagans, this would have been shocking or just absurd. That is why the Apostle Paul described the Good News of Jesus Christ as folly or foolishness to the Greeks. The gospel, after all, does go against our common experience of life.

Think of how the vast majority of this planet's inhabitants experience life: inescapable poverty, high infant mortality, recurrent famine, fatal epidemics, natural disasters, and deadly wars. Think of Congo, Tibet, North Korea, Albania, all recently in the news. Even in affluent Europe and North America, how few think of life as happy. Why would we have such a therapeutically informed culture if we were so happy? To quote the best selling self-help book of all time: "Life is difficult."[1] To proclaim that God is love goes against common experience.

Nevertheless, we persist. "God is love and where true love is, God is there," we sometimes sing. We proclaim that transcending the world of common experience, transcending and penetrating it, is the pervasive divine love. Perhaps today we proclaim this too glibly. Perhaps we sentimentalize this love. Perhaps we, when things seem to be going all right for ourselves, forget that this is not the case for everyone, and, at times in all our lives, will not be the case for us.

To proclaim that "God is love" is counterintuitive. To believe such is to commit us to a countercultural, even a radical confession; or it is escapist fantasy of the highest order, sentimentalist claptrap, the opiate of the masses. It is one or the other. There is no middle ground here, either we are the bearers of a new truth about God and the world or we above all are to be pitied as the greatest of fools. That is the way of the gospel. We are bearers of the message that God is for us, God is with us, God cares for us, and, yes, God loves us. This message should strike us, and does strike pagans, ancient or modern, as a message so good as to border on folly.

But for Christ, this gospel of ours would be folly. In Christ, God brought divine love to our common experience. Not to trick us, to make sport of us, as did the pagan gods; but to join us, to live our common human experience, to suffer, to die, all out of love. And to rise again to show that nothing, not even death, can extinguish this love. That is our hope, our calling, and our mission.

For, you see, the pagans, both ancient and modern, do get something right about faith after all. To get involved with God makes a claim on one's life. Perhaps they understand this better than many of us in the church do. We tend to domesticate the belief that God is love, and forget what this implies about our lives.

To get involved with God makes us vulnerable to God, although our God is not vindictive or cruel, but pure love. We are vulnerable because we must open ourselves up to love and be loved. Our Epistle reads: "Those who say, 'I love God,' and hate their brothers or sisters, are liars; for those who do not love a brother or sister whom they have seen, cannot love God whom they have not seen."[2] "This is my commandment," Jesus says, "that you love one another as I have loved you."[3]

Our mission is to lift up love, as the hidden key to life, now revealed in Jesus Christ—to see all love for anyone or anything as the love of God, to name all love as God's, to be drawn to this love, and to reflect it for the world. For to say "God is love" is bold, even bordering on folly. How will anyone believe it unless they see it in us, in the church? How will anyone be convinced that beneath the pain and suffering of common experience flows the divine love, unless we live that way? May we love because God first loved us. May we then boldly love each other by that grace.

Stephen E. Carlson is Rector of Harcourt Parish,
Church of the Holy Spirit, Kenyon College, in Gambier, Ohio.

---

1. M. Scott Peck, *The Road Less Traveled: A New Psychology of Love, Traditional Values and Spiritual Growth* (New York: Simon and Schuster, 1978).

2. 1 John 4:20.

3. John 15:12.

FEAST OF PENTECOST

Reversals

Acts 2:1–11
Jamie Hamilton

PENTECOST is about reversals. What was once is no longer. What was doomed has been redeemed. What was desolation has become restoration. What was dead has come alive.

Peter is preaching about visions and dreams and hopes. He is no longer sinking in water too deep for him to navigate. Peter is preaching in the center of the city square—on the steps, facing the tongues of the world. He is no longer sealed away in a locked room, isolated and alone, frightened for his very life. Peter is preaching Christ crucified, Christ resurrected. He is no longer denying his Lord as the cock crows. Peter is preaching about the grace of God's forgiveness and the power of God's love. He is no longer held in by the guilt of his weaknesses, fears, and limitations. Peter is moved by the Holy Spirit. He is alive, twirling within the wind of God's presence; and, as the tongues of fire descend upon the tongues of the world, no one will ever be the same again. The incarnation of God's Spirit is no longer limited to Jesus. They and we have become the new creation. God's Spirit dwells in all of us!

The tongues of the world hear, listen, and receive the Word of the Holy Spirit as it sears their bodies, and ours, with fire. The Word of God became flesh, and now the Word of God becomes our flesh. We are alive, just like the world, with God's Spirit. What was once is no longer. Such a reversal! The tower of Babel comes crashing down. Our talk becomes comprehensible, understood, and celebrated. A new creation is afoot. The creation of the world, the creation of Jesus, and now the creation of us, alive with the breath of the Holy Spirit.

Pentecost is a time to remember times when we have felt the Spirit of God descend upon us. Pentecost is a time to remember when words have become flesh.

I was in first grade, Catholic school, pre-Vatican II at the School of the Blessed Sacrament. We were forty kids, five rows of eight in an enormous room with large windows, and in the center of light that streamed into the room was SISTER. Imagine calling your teacher "sister." It sounds so comforting, like "girl-friend," like we were all on a first name basis with her. But, of course, it was not like that. This was SISTER. She was huge, bigger than life, with her white alb of many, many folds. She wore sandals and black socks. A cincture was roped around her middle and as she explained often to us, it meant that she was tied to Christ, bound by God for God. She wore a cross that resembled the branding iron my father used on our cattle. Did I think of that on my own? Probably not. SISTER told us we were all branded by God. Her rosary beads were looped through her cincture on her right side for easy access. SISTER ruled with an iron fist, and I was afraid of her. Soon those rosary beads took on the outline of a holster. Any minute, I thought, SISTER was going to pull out her gun, a quick draw from the holster of rosary beads, and it would be curtains for all of us.

One day during recess, I shared my gun image with my best friend. "How could you say such a thing, accuse a Sister like that. Why, it must be a mortal sin. You need to confess it, because if you die tomorrow, you will go to hell." Just then SISTER went by us, and I watched my friend as her eyes focused on the holster gun rosary beads. And she began to laugh, really laugh, and then I began to laugh, really laugh. And in our song of glee, with tears streaming down our faces, we imagined SISTER pulling out a gun. How silly! And in the midst of benches, and swings, and slides and sand, my words became flesh. I was no longer afraid of SISTER. The weight of her alb lifted off my back. I felt free.

Pentecost is about transforming fear into courage. About God's Word of power and love taking on flesh and becoming alive. And it happens in our everyday talk and walk.

I am still in first grade.

We were celebrating Easter Week at school with an art project. SISTER had stacks of colored paper and markers and we were to draw a picture for Easter. I hated drawing. I passed up the markers, grabbed many sheets of the colored paper and some glue and sat back at my desk. There were no scissors, but that didn't stop me. I was on a mission, so focused was I, as I ripped the paper into strips and began to construct Mary prostrate at the cross of Jesus. Not an Easter scene! I must have been attracted to the agony. Was I realizing that my father drank too much? I don't know; all I remember was how intense this art project became for me. I blocked out everything, as I ripped Mary's face out and placed it in the dirt. SISTER knelt at my desk. That never happened! She was face to face with me. I could feel her breath.

"Jamie, do you want to become a nun?" Of course, I heard, "Do you want to become me?" My *No* was screaming inside of me, but I kept it in. I was speechless.

I wish I could see her now. Tell her that I am a priest. Sister, did you see something so long ago? Some hint, some clue to my future calling? What did you see, Sister? What was I doing? Was I Mary at the foot of the cross? Somehow trying to deal with all that was hurting my six tender years?

She saw me; she heard me. How could she? Her habit covered her ears: "Blinders for Christ," she called her covering. And yet, she did hear me. The author of my life was speaking out. Even her blinders couldn't keep her from seeing.

"It's a beautiful piece, Jamie. Save it." Her words became flesh. I felt heard, and my pain honored. She had touched me.

Pentecost is about the power for us to become community. No matter how awkward, unlikely, unbelievable it may be, God transforms us so that we can be blessed by our reaching out. Our listening makes a difference.

I am fifteen.

My mother, who was on the parish council, came home one day from church and said, "That's it. I'm quitting. I didn't ask Jesus to die for my sins, so it's not my fault he died. I don't need saving, thank you, anyway." And that was it; she did not return.

Twenty years later and I am in the process of becoming a priest.

"How can you believe that Jesus died for our sins?" my mother asked me one quiet afternoon while I was packing to go back home.

"Maybe Jesus died because of our sins."

"I don't believe in sin."

"Mom, how can you not believe in sin? I sin every day. I can't love my loved ones as fully as I desire. I hold grudges. It's hard for me to forgive. Everything falls under my scrutiny. I love to be in control. I don't want to be vulnerable, I am afraid of my weaknesses, and if I had lived during the Holocaust, I probably wouldn't have had the courage to defy Hitler. Kierkegaard tells us that the greatest despair is not knowing you are in despair. Well, maybe the greatest sin is not knowing you are in sin."

With my speech over, I looked over her way. Her face was fallen, and she had retreated. End of conversation. I thought to myself, "Well, there is another sin, my arrogance. Maybe I should try listening."

"Mom, I'm sorry, tell me what sin means for you."

"It means one thing: that I am not worthy of God's grace. But I am worthy. God would not have created me if I weren't worthy. And it's not dependent on my ability to repent, accept, or acknowledge God. From the very beginning, the very beginning of creation, I have been God's child, and I always will be God's child."

Reversal. Pentecost is about not having to love first. We love because God loved us first. We are God's children. And we can make church happen.

I remember the first time I was called a child of God.

"My dear child of God, come here, come here." I was taking consecrated Eucharist to patients of the leukemia floor of Fred Hutchinson Cancer Center. She was dying. The bone marrow transplant was not taking.

"Please, come all the way in. I want you to sit next to me." She was in an isolation room, walled off completely by clear plastic. To go in meant I had to put on the "moon suit." Dressed in hat, mask, gown, gloves, and paper boots, I unzipped the wall and stepped in. As I zipped back the wall, claustrophobia grabbed my throat, but I moved to the chair next to her bed. As I ripped open the hermetically sealed host and placed it on the napkin, I asked her how she was.

"I'm dying. I've just said good-bye to my two little girls. Soon, it will be the last time. Today I want to pray with you that I will be strong for them, I so badly want to be able to be the way God would want me to be." I began to cry. I was so embarrassed. "I shouldn't be the one crying, you should be." She reached out and held my hand and pointed to the Eucharist and then to me. "Jesus does not have to be understood to be felt. Jesus is here."

And then it hit me. I was in her tomb. She would be dead within a week. She had reached across the chasm, from the edge of her death, clasped my gloved hand, and touched life into me through all the layers of protection. The walls came tumbling down, as she transformed her tomb right before my eyes into the womb of Christ.

God's love is greater than sin . . . greater than death. God's love is like the rush of wind swirling all around us. Always with us; and not even death will do us part. Pentecost is about rocks being rolled away, walls tumbling down, and fire searing and sealing us with the Spirit of God. The Word becomes flesh. The Author of our life lives by the grace of the Holy Spirit dwelling in each and every one of us.

Mystery does not have to be understood to be felt.

Jamie Hamilton is Chaplain at Phillips Exeter Academy,
Exeter, New Hampshire.

TRINITY SUNDAY

God, the Unspeakable Intimate Fire

Exodus 3:1–6
Susan M. Smith

THIS IS Trinity Sunday. Not usually a preacher's favorite, for the trinity is really a difficult concept. Do we not believe in *one* God? A three-in-one God can seem confusing, almost like three gods. Some have been tempted by the Unitarian approach. If there is a divinity, there is only *One*. Why must we Christians live with the complication of three in one?

There is no treatise in Scripture on the doctrine of the trinity, no nice explanation in one of Paul's letters for us to read. The trinitarian formula appears in Scripture only once, in Matthew 28, the Great Commission, when Jesus commands the disciples to go forth, baptizing *in the name of the Father, and of the Son, and of the Holy Spirit*. And this is how we baptized our four young people here last week at Pentecost. But what did we mean when we did that? The doctrine of the trinity, as we know it, was not even formulated until the fourth century, by the Cappadocians, St. Gregory of Nyssa, St. Gregory of Nazianzus, and St. Basil—and there was a sister in there, Macrina.

So why are we trinitarian? Why is it so important to us to affirm God as three persons? The story of Moses at the burning bush might give us some clues as to the meaning of this central doctrine of our faith.

> *... The angel of the* LORD *appeared to [Moses] in a flame of fire out of a bush; he looked, and the bush was blazing, yet it was not consumed. Then Moses said, "I must turn aside and look at this great sight, and see why the bush is not burned up." When the* LORD *saw that he had turned aside to see, God called to him out of the bush, "Moses, Moses!" And he said, "Here I am." Then [the* LORD] *said, "Come no closer! Remove the sandals from your feet, for the place on which you are standing is holy ground." ... And Moses hid his face, for he was afraid to look at God.*[1]

What do we hear in this familiar but very strange story? First, that God is the God of the universe, the God who creates the heavens and the earth out of nothing—the awesome, unspeakable God, whose face we cannot look upon and live. Yet this very God reveals Godself in an ordinary bush! Moses has this theophany, an experience of the presence of God, in a simple shrub. If it were in Alaska it could be in a clump of fireweed or in a dandelion patch in our front yard. How do we take account of the Holy Creator appearing in something so common?

This is the God of huge power, of glaciers and volcanoes, who makes the fiery sun out of tiny hydrogen atoms, the God of breathtaking beauty and mysterious oceans, three-foot snowfalls, and earthquakes. Yet this God is so subtle that Moses has to *turn aside* to have this encounter. It is as though Moses sees a flicker in his peripheral vision, and almost misses it. If he had been focused on his list for the day, keeping only his own agenda in mind, he wouldn't even have noticed such a subtle invitation coming from the side, such a quiet, indirect invitation to a divine encounter. It's a little frightening to think that if we're going too fast, we could miss God! What kind of God is this? How do we take account of the Holy Creator who is both dramatic and subtle, powerful and peripheral?

If we read on, we find Moses, in unimaginable boldness, asking God's name. "So, if I do go to Egypt to free your people from Pharaoh, who shall I say sent me? What is your name?" And God responds with the unpronounceable tetragrammaton, which comes from the Hebrew verb "to be." It can be translated "I Am Who I Am" or "The One Who Is" or "I will be with you there; as Who I Am, will I be with you." How do we account for the Holy Creator whose name is incomprehensible, and has to do with very being—yet even so, who shares the intimacy of the holy name with Moses, a common shepherd? We can't except by understanding one God, to be encountered in two different ways, as Creator and as incarnate redeemer.

In Moses' story we encounter the awesome, infinite Holy Creator. But we also encounter a God who is ordinary, subtle, intimate—attributes of God we Christians best know in Jesus Christ. Lest we take this intimacy and presence-in-the-ordinary for granted, we would do well to remember just how counter-cultural and mentally scandalous it is to dare such closeness with the Holy One.

Have you ever heard the song Bette Midler sings, called *From a Distance*? On the one hand, it's a beautiful song, inviting us to perceive what seem like grave problems from the perspective of the spaceship that took the picture of our lovely planet—to take a kind of "God's-eye" perspective on ourselves. But one of the lines in it is "God is watching us from a distance." I agree with the song's invitation to pay attention to our actions, and to keep our perspective. But the doctrine of the trinity teaches us is that ours is not a God who relates to us "from a distance." Yes, God is transcendent, reaching beyond space and matter. Yet this God who is beyond the capacity of the human mind to comprehend is the same God who wants intimacy with us, who will come to Moses in a common plant. This God who is above all and beyond all, mystery inaccessible, also comes to us in specific time and space. The invisible God is made visible in the humanity of Christ. God can limit Godself by time and culture, can experience longing and joy, even suffering and death, and yet remain God.

This God wants intimacy with us. God has squeezed the divine essence into humanity, in Christ Jesus, to be like us, with us, for us. These finite bodies that get sick, that don't function, that smell and leak, that struggle to get along with one another—it is through these bodies, on ordinary yet holy ground, that God seeks intimacy with us. It is almost too much to imagine! This is the mystery of God in Christ. It's almost too much to hold together.

You may have heard of Catherine LaCugna's important essay on the trinity called *God for Us*.[2] In the West, she says, we try to understand by analogy. St. Augustine's metaphor for the trinity was Lover, Beloved, and Love itself. This is a helpful analogy for apprehending the three-way relationship in the one God. In the East, however, the attempt to understand God usually stops the mind in its tracks and results in silence. Any metaphor is regarded as more *unlike* God than *like* God.

The Holy Spirit has no shape, but blows where it will. The Eastern Church constantly acknowledges the breath-giving presence of the Spirit. In the West, the Holy Spirit gets left out a lot. We tend to pray to God the Father through Jesus Christ, our Lord. This, however, is a "di-nity." The ancient way to pray, still emphasized in the Eastern church, is *to the Father through Christ in the power of the Holy Spirit*.

The Council of Nicea generated a creed to affirm this trinitarian relationship. In the West, however, the Nicene Creed was changed in the eighth century to combat Arian Christians who did not affirm that the incarnate God in Christ was the same as the awesome Creator God. The Western Creed claimed that the Holy Spirit proceeded from the Father and the Son (instead of just the Father). That elevated the position of the Son, but made the Holy Spirit a kind of second-class extra. We still feel the effects of this. Perhaps it is to help us regrasp the wholeness of God that our readings today all include the Holy Spirit.

For the Holy Spirit draws us to godliness. God does not stop with creating out of infinite love and power, but is also self-limiting in space and matter to have intimacy with us. This same God wants us to be like God. God came to be like us, that we might be like God. We are called to be deified, christified, sanctified—incarnate where we are, how we are, to see and to *be* the holy in the ordinary.

Who can imagine this? Yet if we dare, we notice, in the background, perhaps—in our peripheral vision—those moments when we have been like God for someone. When, in this conversation, that moment of relationship with friend or stranger—we have been the presence of God for someone. Through the Holy Spirit we encounter holiness—within ourselves, as well as outside ourselves.

The central concern of the doctrine of the trinity is not to point to a numerical mystery but rather to name the God who redeems us in Christ and deifies us through the Holy Spirit. God became like human beings so that we could become like God. We aren't supposed to stop at worshiping God; we are supposed to be deified, sanctified, made holy. As Catherine LaCugna and others suggest, Eastern theology, from the patristic period to the present, has described salvation as "deification" (theosis). Deification means participating in the very life of God, being made like Christ; for through Christ we are made sharers in the divine nature (2 Peter 1:4).

I had an experience yesterday that gave me an intimation of this mysterious reality and this sacred process. It helped me imagine how we could be "like God" in the power of the Holy Spirit. Last week the new native hospital down the street was dedicated. Next weekend, the patients will all be moved from the old Alaska Native Medicine Center to the new one. But this Friday and Saturday, there was a twenty-four-hour purification and memorial service for the old hospital—a celebration of the thousands of people born there and healed there over its fifty-three-year history. A memorial. A time of grieving for the two to three thousand persons who died there, and a chance for their spirits to be released.

The chairs were set up outside very much like we are here, in a circle, with a purifying fire in the middle—a fire, symbol of the Holy Spirit, of refining and cleansing. There were many people who spoke, who sang, who offered prayers and shared stories.

After I had been there some hours, I noticed that there was a man whose job was to keep the fire going. He was not listed on the agenda; he was in the background. Only gradually, from the side, did his presence and his actions come into my consciousness.

He fed the fire. But not just to keep the *fire* going. He fed it at spiritually significant times. There were logs on the four sides of the fire. When some person seemed particularly moved at the time of his or her sharing, the fire-keeper would come forward during their speaking. He would lift up a log from each of the Four Directions and place each one in the fire. And after a person had finished, he would stand at each corner, lift his head to the heavens, and blow his whistle. Sometimes everyone would wait until he finished; other times, speakers would continue through his whistle-blowing. He had a staff to poke the logs. It had two feathers on the top, one of which was an eagle feather.

One time, a speaker introduced his daughter to sing a song. She came to the microphone, looked out over all those people, started to sing—and melted into tears. The firekeeper immediately came forward and fed the fire. Then he followed her over to her seat and gave her a big hug.

Then she came forward again. This time she got through the whole song. It was lovely and short. She sang it a second time, gesturing for support to the group. Everyone stood and many sang with her. When she finished, the firekeeper walked around the fire with his stick. It was as though he was gathering up the smoke from around the fire. He went to her and brushed her up and down. It looked like he was blessing her.

Later, he told his own story, and how he had stayed up all night tending the fire, drumming, and chanting. "I'm doing this," he said tenderly, "to comfort you. I'm doing this to *comfort* you. I want you to know how much I care."

Do you suppose that we might be able to cultivate a bit of distance from our agendas and our lists, a bit of space to notice when the firekeepers are feeding the flames of our passion, the energy of God that never forsakes us, that comforts and strengthens us? Is it possible for us to attend to our peripheral vision, to those faint sounds of birdsong in the background, to those elusive fragrances, that might well be God, the Holy One, coming to us in ordinary space and matter, longing for an intimate encounter? Let us be ready to notice the Spirit of God in a burning bush, to turn aside for an encounter with the mysterious, intimate God who comes to us, so that in the power of the trinity, we ourselves may be made holy!

Susan M. Smith is a doctoral candidate in liturgy at the Graduate Theological Union, Berkeley, California. This sermon was preached while she served at Saint Mary's Church, Anchorage, Alaska.

---

1. Exodus 3:1–6.

2. *God for Us: The Trinity and Christian Life* (San Francisco: Harper San Francisco, 1991). The basic ideas are summarized in a helpful article called "The Trinitarian Mystery of God," *Systematic Theology: Roman Catholic Perspectives,* vol. 1, ed. Francis Schussler Fiorenza and John P. Gavin (Minneapolis: Fortress Press, 1991).

PROPER FOUR

A Day for Being

Deuteronomy 5:6–21; Mark 2:23–28
Susan W. Klein

SUNDAY was still the Sabbath in the 1950s, when I was growing up in the Midwest. Those were the days when everyone was Catholic, Protestant, or Jew. And except for the Jews, most everyone else went to church on Sunday morning. In deference to that nearly two-thousand-year-old tradition, the whole American culture shut down.

Mark Twain once observed that there was "nothing as long as a Protestant Sunday." I knew children who had church, some form of it, all day. That's probably the kind of Sunday Twain is talking about. Our family's routine was as fixed as the stars in the sky. We ate breakfast together and walked to church, or drove, if we were late or it was too cold. We stayed there for choir practice, Sunday school, and church, then came home for lunch. In the afternoons we played or did something together as a family. In the evening, my grandparents usually came over for dinner. Afterwards was homework. After we bought a black-and-white TV, we watched Ed Sullivan, or something else exciting. Then bath and bed. Nothing very strenuous or eventful ever happened on Sunday. Sometimes it did seem long.

But that was the point. It was a day for being, not for doing, and that was part of the gift of the day called Sunday. It was not a day for errands and shopping, because everything except the local deli was closed. It was not a day for working, because all of the businesses were closed. It was not a day for soccer games, birthday parties, swim team practice, especially in the mornings. No one would have come. Everyone was in church, or pretending to be.

Although in my childhood, Sunday, not Saturday, was the Sabbath, the whole culture inherited its understanding of the Sabbath from Judaism. The way we spent our Sundays was very similar to how good Jews had been keeping the Sabbath for several thousand years. Within Judaism the Sabbath teachings were among the most central. A good Jew kept the Sabbath as a way of honoring God, as a way of remembering God, as a way of renewing the human side of the God-human covenant. Rituals, prayers, and songs expressed the teachings and spirituality of Judaism. All of the Gospels say that Jesus went to the synagogue on the Sabbath where he is shown teaching.

Within Judaism, because no one was supposed to do any work on the Sabbath, there was no hierarchy, no system of oppression. On the Sabbath, there were no masters and slaves; no bosses and servants. It was a day of radical equality as each person received the same gift of twenty-four hours of time. On one day of the week, the whole society experienced a powerful sense of human solidarity and community. That was pretty much the way it was, too, when I was growing up.

I am not nostalgic about those times, really. Our culture is pluralistic now with Buddhist, Muslim, and Hindu working and living alongside Catholic, Protestant, and Jew. The pluralism of our society means that there is no uniformity about keeping the Sabbath. Nothing external to us will help us keep the Sabbath anymore. It was easier in the '50s. Now we must do it on our own, and we must defend to others our choice to worship. We must take more responsibility for and be more intentional about the Sabbath. Today if the Sabbath, Sunday, is to be a holy day of worship and rest, we need to make that a priority. And in a funny way, that is what Jesus is saying and doing when he concludes his incident with the Pharisees by saying, "The sabbath was made for humankind, and not humankind for the sabbath."[1]

In Jesus' day, the keeping the Sabbath for the Jews was governed by a multitude of laws, all of which were respected in Palestine by the Romans. A Jew could get into trouble with the religious authorities if he or she were to break any of the Sabbath laws. Above all one was to do no work on the Sabbath, and that included doing anything that required work, like fanning, cooking, and selling. One was not even supposed to help anyone in need.

On the particular Sabbath that Mark's Gospel describes, Jesus breaks the laws of the Sabbath by allowing his disciples to pluck heads of grain to feed themselves. Technically, they are reaping, an activity forbidden on the Sabbath. But Jesus sees what they are doing as a part of keeping the Sabbath. They are hungry. They are being fed. The keeping of the Sabbath needs to take into account human need, human hunger, and the laws must be widened, liberalized to include what matters to humankind.

This highly symbolic story sets the tone for much of what Jesus' ministry is all about. In no way should we see Jesus as recommending that the secularized weekend replace the religious and cultural observances of Judaism. Jesus is not telling his disciples *not* to keep the Sabbath. He is not diminishing the importance of the Sabbath, nor recommending that it be abolished. He is allowing it to be humanized. He is allowing flexibility in the keeping of the Sabbath, based on human need. He knows that on the Sabbath people need to be fed, with physical and with spiritual food, and he allows the laws protecting the Sabbath to be broadened to accommodate human hunger.

This action and this teaching of Jesus speak in obvious ways to our understanding of the Sabbath. Both underscore that the Sabbath was given for us— as humans—to feed human hunger. We are hungry for many things. We are in need of many things. We need many little things constantly like food, water, and shelter. We also need the great things. We need God's love, God's presence. We need to feel a sense of holiness, sacredness in our lives. We need regular, weekly contact with God's people in community.

And that is the point of our coming together, sharing the meal of God we call the Eucharist each week. There are very few rules that govern it. You need a celebrant, a priest or bishop. You need people who are baptized. You need a prayer, bread, and wine. You need to have a little faith. You don't have to be confirmed. You don't have to dress up, wearing hats and gloves, suits and ties. But you do have to be here. No one can be fed in absentia. Since my middle twenties, I can probably count on one hand the Sundays when I have not received the Eucharist. It's not because I have to. It's not even because it is commanded. It is because I need to receive. On the Sabbath, amazing things have happened to me.

Three years ago, while on vacation, I broke my back in an accident. The next Sunday, wearing a back brace, kept from screaming by a very heavy dose of painkillers, I went to the local parish church with my family at eight o'clock. By noon a priest from my home diocese had called me at our resort to see how I was. I was shocked to hear his voice asking me about the accident. What was the connection? Also on vacation, he had come to the same little parish in the middle of resort country at the ten o'clock service and heard the lector praying for me. During coffee hour, the local rector, whom I had met earlier that morning, filled my friend in on all the details. That Sunday I was fed twice, once in the Eucharist and once in friendship; a Sabbath meal with double helpings.

After we are fed, though, the Spirit of Jesus continues to work in us. We often apply his teachings about the Sabbath to other areas of life. Whenever rules and laws—whether in the secular or sacred areas of life—fail to take into account human need, Jesus gives us a clear model for change, for reform. And Jesus' disciples have been breaking the law in his name ever since. Many of his disciples broke the laws of slavery, broke the laws governing segregation, in order to fulfill the Spirit of God's love and mercy. When laws violate the spirit of compassion and respect for all human life, Jesus gives his disciples the freedom and often the courage to break them.

Being a Christian in today's world is not easy. Living into the Sabbath takes discipline, courage sometimes, as we resist the pressures to conform to secularization—to say to one's boss, "I'm sorry, I go to church on Sunday morning. I can't come to that meeting." It may be difficult to say to one's friend, "No, I can't have breakfast with you on Sunday, I need to be with my faith community." That may be threatening. But as we feel the power of new life, as we know we are being fed, week after week, by God's Word and sacrament and by God's people in love and friendship, keeping the Sabbath is what we know we need in order to live.

Paul in one of his letters to the Corinthians[2] gives them an extraordinary image of themselves. He says that they have the treasure of God—his light, his glory—in clay pots, earthen vessels. We often seem very flawed, very cracked, but through those flaws and cracks, God's light is able to shine. Sometimes all we see is the aging, flawed, cracked bowl. We forget to see the light shining through it. It is the work of the Sabbath to help us see who we are.

The Sabbath was made for us. It is a gift for the living of our lives. Through it the sacred, transcendent Spirit of the living God in the Risen Christ enters more fully into our spirit, making us more the creatures we are called to be. Though the world goes compulsively on, more and more frenetic each day, let us keep the Sabbath, a time for being, for seeing, a time made holy, a time to receive, a time to reflect, a time to be fed.

The world won't keep the Sabbath for me anymore. But I will keep it for the world and hold it as an open invitation. Let all who are hungry enter this door and be fed.

Susan W. Klein is Rector of Saint Aiden's Church, Malibu, California.

---

1. Mark 2:27b.
2. 2 Corinthians 4:7–12.

PROPER EIGHT

Risks in Seeking Healing: Two Case Studies
Mark 5:21–43
Rosalind Brown

IF ANY OF YOU have watched someone you love become sicker and sicker while medical help is ineffective, or been stuck in traffic when trying to get someone to the emergency room, you will have some idea of how Jairus felt in the Gospel we hear today. His twelve-year-old daughter was ill. He could do nothing about it himself, and he was powerless to stop his daughter from dying. A tragic situation for any parent. We can imagine the scene at home as he left his wife with their daughter, and rushed off for help in one last, desperate attempt to save her life.

This was one of my favorite Bible stories as a child, perhaps because as a child I could identify with the fact that Jesus helped a little girl. But today I want to look at the Gospel story through the eyes of some of the adults involved—Jairus and the woman who interrupted his mission to get help.

We'll start with Jairus, the leader of the local synagogue either in Capernaum or one of the other small coastal towns on the Sea of Galilee. Why is it significant to know that he was a synagogue leader? That meant he was a lay man, with good knowledge of the Torah, the law, and a respected member of the local community. In Mark's Gospel Jesus has already had two rather dramatic encounters in the synagogue, and if they didn't take place in Jairus's synagogue it is quite probable that he had heard about them. In the first episode, Jesus had been confronted by a man with an unclean spirit who interrupted his teaching. Jesus cast out the unclean spirit in a noisy episode, leaving the man healed and everyone astounded. That evening people were brought to the house where

Jesus was staying, and he healed them. Then Mark tells us that the religious leaders criticized Jesus' disciples for plucking grain on the Sabbath, an act that constituted work. Jesus directly challenged them by healing a man with a withered hand in the synagogue on the Sabbath.

So Jairus knew that Jesus was able to heal, but also that he was in some trouble with the religious authorities because of it. So Jairus was on dangerous ground in asking for Jesus to come and help. But what really made matters worse for him, what put his standing on the line, was the fact that Jesus had just come from the other side of the Sea of Galilee—that was gentile territory. There Jesus had healed a man described as demon-possessed, and apparently let the demon enter a herd of pigs. Jairus and his fellow Jews would have been horrified that Jesus had been to gentile territory, associating with a demon-possessed man and a pig keeper. All of this would make Jesus unclean in their eyes.

So Jairus risks his reputation by going to Jesus for help. His love for his daughter wins out. He goes, falls at Jesus' feet, and begs him to come and help. This is not what people would expect of their synagogue leader. It's a bit like the Senior Warden falling down at the feet of a revivalist preacher who has wandered into town. But Jairus seems beyond caring about his reputation. He only knows that Jesus has healed people and believes that he can heal his daughter.

Do we miss out on God's care for us in our need because we are we too embarrassed at times by what our friends will think if we ask in public?

Then there is the interruption—Mark indicates that there is a crowd around Jesus, so progress was probably slow, surely raising Jairus's anxiety. Suddenly Jesus stops and asks the ridiculous question, "Who touched me?" Can you imagine Jairus's frustration as precious time slips away? But Jesus persists, and so we have the story of the woman with the twelve-year hemorrhage.

She has spent all she had on fruitless visits to doctors and has probably suffered a lot along the way. Anyone losing blood in this way is physically weak. Simple tasks take a lot more energy. This is in the days before iron tablets, and she had been like this for twelve years.

But in addition to the medical problem, she faces exclusion from normal society because of it. According to the law, a woman was unclean during her monthly period and the week thereafter. She was essentially cut off from society for the duration, since anything or anyone she touched became unclean until evening. Then it or they had to be purified by bathing—in a culture where water was a precious commodity and not to be wasted on frequent washing. Any man sleeping with her during that time was unclean for seven days. Would a husband risk that? Had marital life ceased twelve years ago? The fact that she pled her own cause with Jesus suggests that she had been pretty much abandoned, since it was unusual for women to seek help on their own. They were the property of husbands, fathers, or sons.

If she had children, for twelve years—the whole lifetime of Jairus's daughter—she would have been unable to touch them, to hug them at night, to kiss them when they hurt, to sit on their bedding roll to tell them a story, to share normal family interaction with them. Or, if she had, she would have made them ritually unclean, cut off from their friends for the rest of the day and required to undertake rites of purification. What kind of family life would that be?

Perhaps it is not so hard to see why she would have been so desperate for help. According to the law, she made Jesus ritually unclean by touching him. No wonder she reached for his cloak and tried to escape quietly. She risked his wrath and that of the religious leaders and the rest of the crowd who might have touched her accidentally in the crush. This was potentially a very hostile situation. We do not know her name, but Jesus did not let her get away with anonymity. The crowd would certainly expect Jesus to be angry with her. It was an act of bravery for her to own up to the fact that she had touched him.

Surely only the fact that she had felt the healing in her body gave her the courage. But in so doing, and in his response to her—"Daughter, your faith has made you well; go in peace and be healed of your disease"—she knew herself to be accepted back into society. That, as much as the physical healing, was what she needed. She was not just healed physically, she was restored as a whole person to human society.

Isn't that what many people need? They often conceal physical needs or come with a much deeper need to be accepted in a society that creates outcasts.

Mark emphasizes that Jesus is concerned to see that she received that gift as well as the much-needed physical healing. The phrase "Be made well" is actually "Be saved." The Greek word carries the meaning of restoration, making good, being released. Without getting technical, it is significant to know that Mark uses certain words or phrases in this story to describe the woman's suffering that he uses elsewhere only to describe the suffering of Jesus. It is as though Mark wants to impress on his hearers that, although the details were different, Jesus in some way shared this woman's suffering, that he knew what it was to be rejected as she was, to suffer shame and to suffer alone. In a culture that saw women as far less important than men or even boys, Mark is making a radical statement. There are no outcasts in Jesus' world.

Mark also links Jesus' experience with the woman's when he says that both felt something in their bodies when she touched his cloak. She felt healing, and he felt power leave him—a moment between them that the disciples and the crowd knew nothing about. Mark also goes to great lengths to describe not only her ordeal in great detail, but also her persistence in seeking help: she is a determined and faithful woman whose tenacity is rewarded.

Jesus calls her "my daughter." A chapter earlier in Mark, Jesus tells the crowd that whoever does the will of God is his brother and sister and mother. Now he tells her in the hearing of the crowd that she is his daughter. Not only is she part of his family; in seeking healing, she has done the will of God.

By this time Jairus is probably very agitated. Time is short and Jesus has delayed, and now he is ritually unclean. Then comes the message that his daughter is dead, so he shouldn't trouble Jesus any more. Have you ever been discouraged by circumstances that you have prayed about, where God seems to be answering, but then they get worse, and friends suggest that you might as well give up, since God is obviously not going to answer that prayer?

Jesus takes the initiative and tells Jairus not to fear, but only to believe. And Jesus allows only a few close disciples to come with him. Jairus needs to be in the company of people who do not discourage him.

Faithful friends are one of God's gifts, a gift we can be to one another. It is when we are facing hard times, particularly when we are ill or bereaved, that we most need others. We need to rely on the communion of saints, to let others do the praying for us.

When they get to the house, Jesus puts all the mourners outside and risks their contempt by making the apparently ridiculous statement that she is not dead. These are experienced mourners; they know a dead person when they see one. Then Jesus—in an intimate moment with the girl, perhaps trying not to frighten her—takes her hand and calls her "little girl," a name of familial endearment. Mark records the words in Aramaic. The moment must have made an impression on those who heard. And the little girl got up and walked about, astounding everyone. Jesus, ever practical, reminds them that she is probably hungry and needs food. There is nothing ethereal about Jesus; food is often on his agenda!

Where do these stories impact us? You know the answer if you been in the position of any of the characters. But, as a church, I suggest, we need to ask ourselves whether we are in danger of discouraging people—even one another—from seeking Jesus' help. Or do we create an environment where people are encouraged to come forward to ask Jesus for whatever is needed for wholeness and healing?

These stories of two women that Mark intertwines—not only in the telling of the events, but in the common link of twelve years—make a clear statement. However discouraging our circumstances, however afraid we are, however much shame we feel, however shocked we think others might be, however long we have been seeking help, we can reach out and ask Jesus for help either for ourselves or for others.

If we are to reach out and invite others into the church, telling them that they can turn to Jesus in any situation, then we need to make sure that we do so ourselves. Our Sunday worship gives us a particular opportunity week by week, since Jesus has promised to be present wherever two or three are gathered in his name, and especially in the bread and wine of the Eucharist.

Why not use the time, week by week, when you receive the bread and wine as an opportunity to reach out and touch Jesus in faith? Use this time, knowing that we are surrounded by a company of praying people, that we are reaching out to one who has shared our human suffering and knows the deepest needs that we might not dare name for ourselves. Then, like the woman, we can hear with joy and confidence the words: "Go in peace"—Go in peace; your faith has saved you. Go in peace to love and serve the Lord.

*Rosalind Brown is Vicar of St. Thomas' Church,
Canonsburg, Pennsylvania, and a member of
the Community of Celebration.*

Proper Nine (Independence Day)

Perfection in Weakness

2 Corinthians 12:2–10
Malcolm C. Young

"[GOD'S] GRACE is sufficient for you, for [his] power is perfected in weakness." For the last seven days I have repeated these words over and over in my mind. I have spoken this formula to myself as if these words themselves had the power to save. This sentence attracts and repulses me at the same time.

To understand it, I began with its author, Paul. Under extreme hardships this man traveled throughout the ancient world telling the story of Jesus Christ to strangers, to gentiles. For this he was often imprisoned, beaten with rods and the lash nearly to death. Even worse than these dangers, perhaps, were the times when false friends betrayed him. Paul knew suffering. He understood weakness and strength and wrote about them. His writings, which compose one fourth of the New Testament, were the first Scriptures that Christianity produced. This miscellaneous pile of letters to the churches that he founded is older than even the Gospels.

We too easily take for granted their venerated status as Scripture. If you think about it, this means of transmitting religious truth to future generations seems particularly odd. This is not how a right-thinking person would naturally establish a world religion. Instead of systematic statements of faith, instead of a clear description of what is necessary for a Christian to believe, instead of the story of Jesus or a history of the early movement, instead of minutes and agendas from important meetings and conferences, we have these often-obscure letters. There are no mission statements, no long-term planning reports, no personal memoirs, and no organization charts left from those times. Mostly, Paul's letters concern only the petty squabbles and misunderstandings of the fragile early church.

These, the oldest records of Jesus' teachings, have been passed down to us in fragments, as the epitome of incomplete weakness. No one really knows where each letter begins and ends, whom they were written to, or exactly what Paul is talking about. Reading them feels like overhearing one half of a muffled conversation outside of a public phone booth. One can never be completely sure what is going on at the other end, or whether our liberal doses of imagination are enough to read between the lines.

God's strength is perfected in weakness. The letters themselves seem like the most convincing proof of this statement. We may not know many of the details, but Paul is very much on the defensive in his second letter to the Corinthians. Paul's opponents have come to this community that he founded and convinced the people that he is weak, that he lacks courage, that he boasts too much and cannot speak forcefully.

Reading the letter as a whole, one hardly knows whether to feel embarrassed for Paul or amused by his outrageous sense of humor. In today's reading he seems to be boasting in the third person about being caught up into the third heaven. Then he goes on to brag about God's consoling response to his prayers. Finally, he takes the last step over the precipice into the abyss that is either absurdity or profound faith. He says, "I will . . . boast gladly in weakness. . . . For whenever I am weak, then I am strong."[1]

Could this be true not only for Paul but also for us? Could it be that at our most depressed, most incompetent, most wounded, most unlucky, most vulnerable moments we are somehow closer to the strength that belongs to God's children?

This is not an academic question. These days I have been feeling pretty weak. I see a lot of change around me, and I want to know whether this is only a reassuring method of making virtues out of necessities, or if this really is true. I want to know if this is God's truth on the great stage of society and in the more personal and intimate details of my life.

On the weekend of Independence Day we should ask if we see evidence in our civic life that God's power is perfected in weakness. The cynic may point out that nice people finish last in politics. We may not be able to identify many heroes in public life these days. Distrust of government at all levels seems to characterize our age. So where is God operating in all of this weakness?

The famous French deconstructionist and social critic Michel Foucault used to write about weak power and strong power. Weak power is the strength of the neighborhood bully who enforces his will by terrorizing others. It is the force that insecure dictators and bloodthirsty tyrants exert to torture their people into submission. Foucault points out that weak power never lasts and quickly destroys itself.

Strong power, on the other hand, is the power of persuasion. Strong power wins the hearts and souls of people by convincing them of the nobility of the cause. Strong power strives to gain people's respect rather than to subjugate them.

As we look back to the American Revolution, we may have the sense that this democratic experiment was founded on the premise that society works best when its citizens have freedom. Indeed there is a certain strength in a nation that governs by persuasion rather than by force, a nation that exerts its control weakly so that its people can be strong. We all can probably imagine other ways that God's power is perfected in weakness on the great stage of society, but I believe that this truth is more difficult to recognize in our individual lives. Often, the closer I am to real pain and real weakness, the harder it is for me to see evidence of God's strength. I wonder how often we ever see that God's power is perfected in our more ordinary moments of weakness.

The southern, Roman Catholic author Flannery O'Connor understood weakness. In her disturbing, almost grotesque fiction, she never permitted her readers to forget that each of her characters is profoundly subject to sin and never capable of any real nobility before God. She writes about criminals, false prophets, and people with deep physical and psychological wounds, about ignorance, strangeness, racists, and pettiness.

O'Connor herself was sickly all her life and ultimately died at a young age of lupus. In her letters to her closest friends she endorses Paul's observation. She claimed that sickness was not inappropriate, but instructive—that sickness was, in fact, one of God's mercies. This bold woman seemed to believe that God's power is perfected in weakness.[2]

Something within me, though, rebels against these sorts of statements. Try repeating them at the side of a hospital bed, in the presence of real suffering. Many of you have heard me talk about my saintly younger brother Andrew. He patiently followed me around and imitated me as we grew up. He felt determined to play football and rugby despite his small size because he wanted to be more like me. I will never forget riding our bikes home from practice at twilight along the springtime streets of our small town. He has always been so dedicated to everything he loved in life that I almost believed he would live forever.

The saddest moment for me over the last year was when I heard the news that my younger brother had been diagnosed with type A diabetes. This immortal Apollo was suddenly talking about kidney failure, dialysis machines, blindness, impotence, circulatory problems, crippling amputations, heart disease, nerve damage, and nursing homes. Even his boundless energy and love of life could not protect him from the frailty of our biology. There is no happy ending here. It is very hard to see any evidence of God's strength becoming perfected in this weakness.

With all of this in mind, how can we return to Paul's boasting of his weakness without a sense of bitterness? Where is the perfection of God? When one begins to talk about religion it is all too easy to forget the cross. We can be too apt to believe that religion is only for making us feel good rather than an honest search for truth and God. We forget that even Jesus could do no deed of power in his hometown. Even for him religion involved more than merely having his own way.

In America we believe in self-determination, that ultimately we are the ones responsible for our success or failure. We live in such a proud, can-do sort of society that we often think that what matters religiously is only what we do to and for others. We easily come to think that the religious life is coterminous with moral action. But there is more to being a Christian than doing good works. Submitting to God's refining fire must also be part of our piety.

In a genuine life of faith, what is done to us is as important as what we do. "God's rule not only requires [us] to do something to others, but also to have something done to [ourselves]."[3] Often adversity drives us even further into the shell of our egotism. Often it makes us even more likely to lose everything in a sea of "Why-me's." But a Christian cannot be satisfied only with this sort of self-indulgence.

For Christians, in moments of humiliating weakness, we are not so much closer to God as we are further from the ego that obstructs our view of God. In this sense it takes major trauma for any of us to know what it is like to be back home with our God. The sad fact of the matter is that perhaps ultimately, human beings are simply not equipped to have their own way without vastly contributing to their self-destruction. The weakness that interrupts the illusion of our control over our own lives may be the only thing that can help us to see the Father who created us and loves us.

Last night I called my brother late at his office to talk about whether he sees any evidence that God's strength is perfected in weakness. Andrew reminded me of the inconvenience, the discomfort, the mental distress, the indignities, fear, frustration, and the nagging sense of inadequacy that he feels. But he also told me that we are too tempted to depend only on ourselves and that the severer forms of weakness remind us that we can rely only on the Lord. He told me that his failing health has taught him something about the importance of being able to accept our lives just as they are. Only in our moments of weakness can we learn to accept God's will, and look for grace in the sort of life that he has so generously given to us.

Malcolm C. Young is Priest Associate at
St. Anne's Church in Lincoln, Massachusetts.

---

1. 2 Corinthians 1:2:9b, 10b.

2. Flannery O'Connor, *The Habit of Being*, ed. Sally Fitzgerald (New York: Vintage Books, 1980).

3. Richard H. Niebuhr, *History and Culture: Major Unpublished Writings* (New Haven: Yale University Press, 1996), 147.

Proper Ten

Prophetic "Pains" and Plumb Lines

Amos 7:7–15
G. Porter Taylor

PROPHETS are *such pains*. They just refuse to get with the program. Just when things are going smoothly, they start making waves.

Today we heard from Amos. What a *pain* Amos is. Amos lives in the good times of Israel. Jeroboam II is a powerful king. Israel is at peace with her neighbors. The economy is good. People are working. Life is humming along. Things are looking good. And along comes Amos. What *is* his problem? Why can't he get with the program?

Amos's problem is that God has given him a vision, and he cannot get God's vision out of his head. Amos would like to get with the program. He'd like to go back to his sheep and sycamore trees. But he can't. He can't because he no longer sees the world the way he used to. God has showed him how out of kilter Israel is.

"See, I am setting a plumb line in the midst of my people Israel."[1]

A plumb line—a reference point. A way of seeing how our ways are different from God's ways. Prophets give us a way of standing back and appraising our condition.

Our house in Nashville was built in 1924, so nothing was plumb. You could put a marble in the center of any floor and it would roll to the corner. We were constantly in need of a level, an outside authority. Because if we looked only at our environment, everything would look right, but nothing would really be right.

That's Amos. He tells us he is a dresser of sycamore trees. That means he cuts the top of the fruit open. If the fruit is healthy, letting in air makes it ripen sooner and become juicier. If there are insects inside, opening it up gets them out.

Amos is dressing Israel—cutting her open to show what is healthy and what is not.

And what does he find?

Underneath the prosperity and lack of conflict is a people who have forgotten God's command to care for the poor, the defenseless, the little ones of the world. Amos says the law courts only serve the rich. Wealthy merchants are concerned only with their profit and so they exploit the poor.

"They trample the heads of the weak into the dust of the earth and they force the lowly away."[2]

The temples, he says, are only going through the motions, putting on better and better rituals, but not changing people's hearts or their actions.

That's why Amos, like all prophets, is a pain. Because they call us to account.

Well, what about us? What about our world? How does it look when we put it beside God's plumb line?

Our first temptation is to focus on rules of behavior and sins of the flesh. And we could talk about promiscuity or adultery or sex outside marriage or . . . . I always want to rail against violence and the abundance of guns. Or we could go for alcohol and drug abuse. All those are sinful. All lead us away from God's ways.

But I think Amos points us deeper. Amos points us to assumptions we make that are so insidious because they are so hidden. Let me try to get at this with a story:

Once a woman went into a café. She sat at a table for two, ordered coffee, and prepared to eat some cookies she had in her purse. The café was crowded, so a man took the other chair and also ordered coffee. The woman began reading her newspaper, and then she reached over and took a cookie out of the package. She noticed the man took a cookie as well. This upset her, but she kept on reading. After a while she took another cookie. And so did he.

She became angry and glared at the man as he reached over and took the last cookie in the package, smiled, and offered her half of it. The woman was indignant and left in a huff.

As she was paying for her coffee, she noticed that in her purse was her package of unopened cookies.

Let me take this story and mention three hidden sins.

First, we worship things, and we worship people who have things. We talk about obeying the Ten Commandments, but what about the eighth commandment: "Thou shalt not covet"? Our economy is driven by creating desire. Although we have benefited greatly from our economic system, its downside is that it makes us want beyond our needs. Why do we need so many things when there are so many who have no things? Like the woman, we fixate on who owns what, instead of sharing what lies before us. We forget that everything is given to us by God, and so we think we are entitled to these things.

Second, we are so afraid of one another. We think in terms of lawsuits, or being harmed, or being offended. I am all for making people accountable for their behavior. But we are called to see others as children of God, as brothers and sisters and not as threats. We know how to be wise as serpents. But what about innocent as doves?

Like the woman—we don't think there are enough things or love or community, so we are fearful that those next to us will take what we have; we forget that Christ is found in community.

> *We are the boat*
> *We are the sea*
> *I sail in you*
> *You sail in me.*

Finally, we have forgotten our call to sacrifice. What if those cookies really were the woman's? Why not take bread, bless it, break it, and share it?

I don't expect our society to talk about giving up for others. But I expect Christians to. I expect myself to. And how often I fail. How often we fail.

The worship of things. The fear of others. The failure to sacrifice.

We gather together to remember that Jesus Christ is our plumb line. To ask God to be like the man in the café. The one who takes what by God's grace is given to him and shares it with others. So that Christ might join them at the table.

G. Porter Taylor is Rector of St. Gregory the Great Church, Athens, Georgia.

---

1. Amos 7:8b.

2. Amos 2:7a.

I Will Not Contend Forever

Ephesians 2:11–22; Isaiah 57:14–21
Howard W. Whitaker

LINDA was the foster child from hell. Not that the Shermans hadn't thought this out. After all, John was retired from the military, Molly was a nurse. They were mature, caring, Christian people. They had a wonderful family they wanted to share. It could be fun. They and their own children Karl and Katie *had* talked a long time about how hard it was going to be to bring someone else into their family. But it was even harder than they had talked about.

Linda was twelve when she came to live with the Shermans. She looked more like sixteen. She smoked. She drank. She had jewelry hanging out of places on her body that Molly didn't even know you could pierce. ("Doesn't that hurt, dear?")

She had pinup posters of . . . well . . . naked guys. Molly drew the line there and wouldn't let Linda put them up. ("Not in my house!" Molly sniffed.) Linda had wanted a hamster. The Shermans bought her one. She named it Slut. Before you get entirely the wrong idea, the boys at the middle school were simply scared to death of her.

This was understandable, because when Linda got mad—which was frequently—it was like watching *The Incredible Hulk*. Her teeth bared. Her face turned crimson. Her pupils would dilate, making her eyes look like black saucers. Her hair would stand straight up like an animal trying to make itself look bigger. It worked.

She came to the Shermans straight from the hospital. Before the hospital, she had been on the street. Before that she had been living with some relatives who . . . well, that's another story.

One night, John Sherman, a big, tough, retired airborne ranger, sat in my office and cried:

> I can't do this. . . . We really do want to give her a good, safe home, but she's not an adult, she can't just do any damn thing she wants. . . . My kids never gave us this kind of trouble. . . . Now all we do is fight. . . . Everybody ends up taking sides and screaming at each other. . . . That's just not the way my family does things.

It was late. I was tired. Okay. I knew it was not a brilliant, inspired piece of pastoral advice. All I could say was, "You may have to figure out how to love Linda just like she is."

"Easy for you to say," retorted John. "Why don't you let her come live with you and your kids for a while?" He slammed his coffee cup down in the trash-can and stomped out.

Two nights later, we were in the emergency room. Linda had "borrowed" the car, and predictably—and I suppose mercifully—had run it into a tree. No one else was involved. Linda would be okay. The car was totaled. Molly Sherman had waited a long time for one of those big Ford Explorers. It was silver. It had been a twenty-fifth anniversary gift from John.

When I walked in, Linda was screaming, medical apparatus was flying, and nurses were taking cover.

You gonna send me back now? You gonna hit me? Come on, big bad army man. . . . BE all you can be. . . . Mold young minds in the way they should go.

There was dead silence. Molly was softly sobbing. And then John began to cry. And then Linda began to cry. The heavens opened up and then John and Linda and Molly and Karl and Katie all sort of melted into this big glob on the bed. The security guard and I instinctively backed out of the room. God was in that place and we knew we could not gaze on it directly.

I cite my text, from this morning's first lesson from the fifty-seventh chapter of the Prophet Isaiah. God says:

> *"I do not want to be forever accusing*
> *Nor always to be angry*
> *Or the spirit would fail under my onslaught,*
> *The souls that I myself have made."* [1]
> *I struck them, I . . . was angry;*
> *But they kept turning back to their old ways.*
> *I have seen their ways, but I will heal them;*
> *I will lead them and repay them with comfort."* [2]

In other words, God seems to be saying,

> *Look, I've got to try something new here. I've yelled and screamed and struck and smited most of the way through the Old Testament, and it hasn't done me any good. I don't want to contend [KJV] forever. I'm tired of being angry. This is not what I had in mind at Sinai when I said, "Hey, you guys can be my people, and I'll be your God." It was supposed to be fun.*
>
> *I figure, now I'm gonna really teach my people a lesson: I'm going to love them. I'm going to heal them.*

I don't think you can make yourself forgive any more than you can make yourself rest. I think you have to be tired first. Most of us figure out how to love, how to forgive, and how to heal because at some point we begin to hate how it feels to be scared of other people. It gets to be too burdensome to feed our anger; it gets to be too much trouble to figure out how to hurt someone else all the time; we just get too damn tired.

In Isaiah, God decides to forgive and heal . . . not because of some secret, sacred, unobtainable, available-only-to-the-holy attribute, but because *it's just easier.* "I'm *tired* of contending. . . . I'm going to forgive, because it's not creative and godlike to be this way. . . . After a while, it's just easier for me."

Here's the gospel: We don't have to be holier than Moses to forgive. We've just got to be tired of contending.

We can forgive and heal; we can love, because God first loved us. As we have heard this morning, it is in the Word made flesh that God has "broken down the dividing wall, that is, the hostility between us."[3] And, like Linda and her new family, it is in the flesh we have to work that out. It is "not by might, nor by power, but by my spirit, says the LORD of hosts," [4] that healing is allowed to take place.

Howard W. Whitaker is Director of Clinical Pastoral Services
in Chattanooga, Tennessee.

---

1. Isaiah 57:16, NJB.
2. Isaiah 57:17b–18a.
3. Ephesians 2:14b.
4. Zechariah 4:6b.

■ 4

PROPER THIRTEEN

Manna from Heaven

John 6:24–35
Norman R. Runnion

I WAS VISITING a friend on Thursday and she said, "Well, I guess summer is over." How come, I asked? "Because this is July 31st," she said, "and we all know Vermont has two seasons—July and winter."

So now it's August. And the weather continues delightful. Good weather outside of July, you might say, is manna from heaven.

Manna from heaven. It's a real language idiom. A good day on the golf course is manna from heaven. Winning a raffle is manna from heaven. I'll bet this phrase is used over and over again in people's ordinary lives; and I'll also bet that very few people know that it comes from the Bible. Over and over again if you read the Bible, you stumble on an idiom, a common everyday expression, and you say, "I didn't know that came from the Bible." The Bible has an impact on people's lives in thousands of ways.

Manna from heaven. It means the unexpected. The ancient Hebrews were wandering in the wilderness, and they were hungry and complaining, and God gave them food. Real food. And they said, when they saw it, "What's this?" And the Hebrew language phrase for "what's this?" is *manna*. Sometimes I serve up a special dinner dish for our kids, and if they were ancient Hebrews, they would say, "Manna." And I would reply, "Vegetable pizza," or something similar.

Manna is for real. In the Sinai desert today, Arabs eat "manna," and they call it *mann*, with two *n*s, and they say it is a gift from heaven.

Now this may be more than you want to know about manna, but I found it interesting. Manna appears to be a honeydew secretion from two kinds of insects that feed on the sap of the tamarack tree, which is all over the Sinai. The honeydew is rich in three basic sugars and pectin. Most of the moisture evaporates in the dry desert air, and what is left are sticky droplets on the plants or the ground. The Hebrews would pick up this honeydew. It could be boiled in pots or ground into meal and baked into cakes. Among other things, this story from the book of Exodus reminds us once again how resourceful God created men and women.

The wandering Hebrews, by the way, came from civilized Egypt, as our story reminds us, and the phenomenon of the tamarack bush and its honeydew-producing insects would have surprised them. And they thanked God for manna.

The manna story had a profound effect on religious beliefs for thousands of years. It led directly to one of the most famous sayings of Jesus: "I am the bread of life. Whoever comes to me will never be hungry, and whoever believes in me will never be thirsty."[1]

If anything can be called a foundational belief of Christianity, that's it.

As we know from today's great passage from the Gospel of John, Jesus made that statement in reply to questions about manna from heaven. The people surrounding Jesus wanted a tangible sign that he was a man of God. And Jesus said I am the sign. I am the Bread of Life.

Tucked away in the middle of the prayer book, beginning on page 396, is the rite called Communion under Special Circumstances. The form, as the book explains, "is intended for use with those who for reasonable cause cannot be present at a public celebration of the Eucharist." It is the form I use whenever I take communion to the sick.

Significantly enough, the rite begins with four quotations from the Gospel of John. Two of them talk about bread, including the phrase from today's Gospel: "I am the bread of life; whoever comes to me shall not hunger, and whoever believes in me shall never thirst."

Bread and wine are the symbols of life. They are the symbols of healing. Holy Communion has incredible power in people's lives. Last Sunday, I took the power of Holy Communion to Dartmouth Hitchcock Medical Center. I was visiting an old friend from Brattleboro, George Lewis, who was recovering from open-heart surgery. George was Bishop Swenson's assistant at my ordination for the diaconate. Considering our relationship over the years, it was very moving for both of us for me to be present at his bedside with a communion kit. "I am through the operation," he said, "and now I want and need the sacraments." And then he cried. "Jesus was with me during the operation," he said.

Last Thursday I went back to the hospital to visit George and found that he had been discharged and was back in Brattleboro. I was standing in the chaplain's office at the hospital when Penny McClure, the secretary, said, "Oh, Norm, can you help us?" There was an Episcopal patient on the fourth floor, she said, who wanted communion, but there was no one around who could give it to him. "Could you help?" she said. "He really needs it."

I took the portable communion kit from the chaplain's office, and the prayer book with the rite of Communion under Special Circumstances, upstairs. The man, who is in his seventies, was lying face up on the bed with a sheet pulled nearly over his face. He was due to be taken for surgery in half an hour, his wife said. He's from New Hampshire, near Woodstock, and like my friend George Lewis, serves on his church's vestry.

"I've brought communion," I said, and he pulled the sheet away from his face and said, "Thank God." The surgery, he explained, was to try to ease immense pain. "You got here just in time," he said, "because I'm due to go up in a few minutes." It was God's time, not mine.

He couldn't swallow either bread or wine with surgery imminent, and he told his wife, "Don't worry, I'll just touch it to my lips." And he took the bread, and dipped it into the small portable chalice, and brushed the bread of heaven and the cup of salvation against his lips, and he lay back on the pillow, awaiting surgery, with a look of utter peace.

Jesus said, "I am the bread of life; whoever comes to me shall not hunger, and whoever believes in me shall never thirst."

My friend had been given manna from heaven.

Norman R. Runnion is Rector of St. Martin's Church, Fairlee, Vermont.

---

1. John 6:35.

PROPER FOURTEEN

Compassionate Anger

Ephesians 4:25–5:2
Elisabeth Eisenstadt

IF ALL of those inconsiderate drivers would just get off the road, I would have a wonderful time driving to work. Unless I have something I have to buy on Route 30, I take the back roads. Horses nibble grass in lush fields. White-headed cows cluster around bales of hay or sit placidly in their well-kept meadows, thinking great thoughts, or not thinking at all. Charming farmhouses keep a politely disdainful distance from ugly nouveau riche mansions. And I get to cruise past two immaculate golf courses, where neither stifling heat nor pouring rain seems to keep the players from their appointed tee times.

But about half the time, I'm not enjoying the scenery. Instead, I've got some teenager in an extravagant sports car or suburban Indy 500 enthusiast in a Land Rover hovering about two feet from my back bumper. I'm not a particularly timid driver. But why are half of those who share the road with me in such a hurry that they risk my life and that of my child to clock an extra two minutes dropping off *their* child, pulling into the company parking lot, or getting to high school before the morning bell?

Under these conditions do I display saintly forbearance? Do I pray for my tormentors? Do I simply pull over and let them pass? Not likely. My hands clench on the wheel. My eyes narrow. And unless Sian, my daughter, is in the car with me, I use language most unfitting to a woman of the cloth (or anyone who claims to be civilized).

So driving to work, taking a child to school, or merely going to the grocery store, for many of us, becomes an exercise in coping with aggressive anger. Sometimes we are on the giving, and sometimes on the receiving, end. And the aftereffect sticks to us throughout the day like the smell of cheap perfume.

Unless you happen to live in an order of cloistered nuns and don't do the food shopping, you too participate in the culture of deliciously delineated hostility. If you want quick and dirty, just thumb through the front-page stories of our popular tabloids. If you are a little more sophisticated in your taste for revenge, read about the dog-eat-dog world of Congress, or Bill Clinton's love life.

Assert yourself. Express yourself. Allow the real you to emerge. Aren't these the kinds of messages we are always getting in self-help books, in advice columns, in some therapist's offices?

We call it free speech, or freedom of thought, or American free enterprise at its finest.

Self-expression does mean we are free, doesn't it?

How naive do the words of Ephesians sound amidst all this battle cry of freedom to be ourselves: "Therefore each of you must put off falsehood and speak truthfully to his [or her] neighbor, for we are all members of one body. In your anger do not sin. Do not let the sun go down while you are still angry, and do not give the devil a foothold."[1]

This sounds very strange to us, because many Christians, standing up against a culture of indulgence, say that if you are a follower of Jesus the Messiah, you shouldn't get angry at all. Let's show the world, so full of meanness and idolatry, how morally superior we are by putting on sweetness and light all the time. Which is impossible, of course.

We've got a problem, because we do get mad. And sometimes it's hard to disguise. Then we have a couple of choices: Just tell our buddies who will agree with us that so-and-so is a reprobate and a spiritual hypocrite. Or tell the world that we are righteously angry, with good reason, and here's why.

But what is the author of Ephesians telling us to do? First of all, he assumes that we are going to get angry. There's nothing the least bit namby-pamby about the writer of Ephesians. Instead, he seems to say the opposite of what we might prefer to do. Don't pretend, don't evade, and don't gloss over. If you have a bone to pick with your neighbor, do it openly and honestly. Put yourself on the line.

More important than your individual feelings, satisfaction, integrity even, is the good of the community. And if the Christian community is internally broken, if whispers and muttered accusations and quiet knives in the back rend it, then it is living in sin.

It's not easy for us to live into this notion of community. After all, how many of us share a house with an elderly relative anymore? How many of your streets still have block parties? How many of you carpool to work? How many of you live within walking distance of a store or even near a sidewalk?

And we've seen so many mockeries of community in this century, such as communism, that it may blind us to seeing the opposite peril, an unbridled individualism that has crept even into the doors of the church itself.

"Do not let any unwholesome talk come out of your mouths, but only what is helpful for building others up according to their needs, that it may benefit those who listen."[2]

How do we know what unwholesome talk is? All I can say is, I always know it when I hear it coming out of my mouth. It leaves me feeling a bit uneasy, unclean, and ashamed.

So if we are to deal with our anger and malice constructively for the greater good of this church body, we must strip ourselves of destructive habits that eat away at the core of who we are, both alone and together.

But then, what are we to put in their place? A cry out of the dust. An embrace out of the darkness. A love that emerges from time on our knees. An empathy that recognizes in a brother or sister a fellow rock climber rescued from the cliff, a colleague plucked from drowning, another child handed out of a burning house.

"Be kind and compassionate to one another, forgiving each other, just as in Christ God forgave you."[3]

God forgave, and forgives us, the corrosive selfishness that constantly threatens to undermine the very relationships we treasure. God forgave, and forgives us, when we fall short of our expectations. God forgave, and forgives us, when we shut our eyes to the call to inner righteousness, mercy, and humility.

But the very power that forgives sins confessed calls us to new efforts on behalf of those with whom we share our lives. Kindness and compassion must be fed both by our living out the knowledge of God's forgiveness and by our own self-knowledge as his children. We aren't merely teenagers, banging on the door at three in the morning after a little too much to drink. As children of one Father, we are adults, lifting each other out of the quicksand, welcoming each other in the love that springs from shared suffering and shared joy.

That's why you and I are called to build each other up. There's no point in undercutting another Christian, no matter how much you disagree with their theology, or their politics, or their taste in music.

Sometimes that means honest confrontation. Sometimes that means a shared moment of quiet prayer. Sometimes that means a casserole at the door, or a ride to the doctors. If we don't do these things, others will look at us and ask, "On what do *they* base their faith?"

If we do these things, our church will be a place to which the wounded and the strong, the joyous and the mourning ones will come. And they will say, "Child of God, I need a home." And we will say: "Come in. His door is open. Be at peace."

Elisabeth Eisenstadt is Assistant to the Rector, Good Samaritan Church, Paoli, Pennsylvania.

---

1. Ephesians 4:25–27, NIV.

2. Ephesians 4:29, NIV

3. Ephesians 4:32, NIV

PROPER SIXTEEN

Choosing Life

Joshua 24: 1–2a, 14–25; John 6:60–69
Susan E. Goff

Lord, to whom can we go? You have the words of eternal life.

Many of those who followed Jesus were turning away. His teachings about the bread of life, about his flesh being food and his blood being drink, were just too hard. They were scandalous, offensive, cannibalistic, and too bizarre to believe. So followers left Jesus. They stopped following in the way they had begun. Jesus turned to his closest friends, the Twelve, and said, "Do you wish to go, too?" Peter answered for himself and for the others when he said the words we heard this morning: "Lord, to whom can we go? You have the words of eternal life."[1] A time of choice. A turning point. Peter and the Twelve chose life.

". . . Choose today whom you will serve . . . . As for me and my house, we will serve the LORD."[2] Joshua put the choice before the people—Joshua, who was the successor of Moses and leader of Israel when they entered the promised land after hundreds of years of slavery in Egypt and forty years of life in the wilderness. Joshua put the choice before the people, to follow the God they knew in Egypt and came to trust in the wilderness, or to worship the gods of the people in the land they entered. A time of choice. A turning point. Joshua and the Israelites chose life.

Some years ago, eighty-four-year-old Mimi became ill. It was not a serious illness at first, but it was quickly compounded by Mimi's worry, which kept her up all night, and by her atrocious eating habits, particularly her refusal to drink water. Little by little, day by day, she became weaker until her doctors diagnosed Parkinson's disease and Alzheimer's. Her children, desperate for relief from worry about her, put her in a nursing home, just for the weekend, so that they could get some much-needed time away. A time of choice. A turning point.

Dick, a priest in the Episcopal Church, was in his forties and was deeply involved in youth ministry. One of the themes of his discussion with youth was "Misery is optional." As young people shared with him how parents or teachers made them feel angry, upset, or miserable, Dick would teach that no one can make you miserable, for misery is a choice. It is optional. The youth usually didn't understand, but Dick was insistent. Then Dick received the shocking news that he had an inoperable brain tumor. How could he continue to choose life when misery was staring him in the face? How could he continue to believe that misery was optional? A time of choice. A turning point.

And Alice, dear Alice. She was sixteen when she first tried to choose death. I don't know that we can ever understand why a beautiful girl, so full of talent and energy, would try to take her own life. But Alice knew misery. She didn't know how to choose life. She just hadn't had enough years of experience to know how to live. Every day was a turning point for her.

We come to turning points again and again in our lifetimes. We come to times when we must choose between life and death, between delight and misery, between truly being alive and merely existing. God created us for more than mere existence, so God cares passionately and intimately about what we choose. The language used in today's Gospel reading makes this clear.

In the Greek language in which the New Testament was written, there are two words that are translated as life. The first of these is *bios*, from which our words *biology* and *biography* derive. *Bios* refers to duration of life, as in the psalm that says, "A person's life is seventy years." It also refers to the wealth or possessions one accumulates in life, as in the story of the widow who put "her whole life" into the temple treasury. Now life in terms of length of years and what one owns is something we in our age can understand. We live in a society in which people do all they can to extend life, ensuring long duration even at the cost of quality of life. And we often judge the value of another's life by what he or she owns. But *bios* is used only eleven times in the New Testament. There is another word that is used ten times more, the word we heard in the Gospel when Peter said, "You have the words of life." This is *zoe*, from which our word *zoology* derives.

Zoe also has two meanings. At its primary level, it means life as a vital, natural force, as the organic functioning that we share with all plants and animals. It is life as opposed to death. But for human beings, *zoe* means even more. It is life in community with God and others that we enjoy as a gift from God. Life with God and others that we *enjoy*. Delight and wonder, celebration in our relationships with God and with other people—God intends these to be basic to life. This life, the life given to us by God, is more than mere existence. It is fullness of life that rejects fatalism, fullness of life that rejects misery and chooses hope, joy, and wonder.

"Where can we go?" Peter asked Jesus. "You have the words of eternal life." You hold up for us the possibility of delight and hope and vitality and goodness, in this world and in the world to come. We choose that over mere existence, over long duration of life, over wealth. We choose Life.

Mimi in her weakness and confusion could not choose life. She was discouraged and afraid and too weak to fight. But her friends chose life for her. One went and physically carried Mimi from the nursing home and took her to the home of another friend. For weeks friends and members of the church encouraged her, pushed her to eat and drink properly, got her up and took her for walks—until Mimi was strong enough to choose life herself. Then her recovery was remarkable. All symptoms of Parkinson's and Alzheimer's disappeared; the symptoms had been caused by malnutrition and dehydration. Now, at age ninety-four, Mimi still walks the six blocks to church every Sunday where she encourages others, through her witness, to choose life.

Dick continued to believe and to preach that misery is optional. The brain tumor was tenacious, relentless, and horribly painful. No treatments seemed to work. But Dick *lived* every day until he died. He spent time with the young people and others who came to visit him, laughing as they remembered stories, crying over what was happening to Dick, and when the pain and discomfort were too much, just holding hands and praying. Dick truly practiced what he had always preached and never allowed misery to be an option. Dick chose life.

Alice still struggles with misery, with life and death, every day. The only relief she seems to find from the struggle is acting. On stage, Alice can become another person, escaping her own pain for a while. She pours herself into her roles and is full of unjaded talent. She played Jesus in *Godspell* and became deeply challenged by his example, his facing of pain, his self-giving love. She wants to choose to follow him. She wants to choose life. But for now, with the help of a good counselor and friends, it is all she can do to choose to live one day at a time. Alice is still learning how to choose life.

And what of us? What do we choose? Do we choose to be victims of the circumstances of our lives? Do we choose misery, which is ours only if we choose it, no matter what life thrusts upon us? Do we choose delight and wonder and hope, no matter what circumstances life throws our way?

We are people created for life, for the fullness of life in joy and wonder. We are created with the capacity to choose life or not, as we will. God desires life for us, rich, abundant life in this world and in the world to come, life measured not in length or possessions, but in the fullness of relationship with God and with others. God gives us the strength to choose such life for ourselves and for those we love. And God gives us the community that can choose life for us when we cannot choose it for ourselves. God gives us life and wants us to know the fullness of that gift.

So with Peter and the Twelve, with Joshua and the Israelites, with Mimi and her friends, and Dick and Alice, let us choose life-abundant life, delight-filled life, eternal life.

Susan E. Goff is Rector of St. Christopher's Church in Springfield, Virginia.

---

1. John 6:68b.
2. Joshua 24:15, RSV.

PROPER TWENTY-ONE

Stepping out of the Tent

Numbers 11:4–6, 10–16, 24–29; Mark 9:38–43, 45, 47–48
Katherine B. Moorehead

MY FATHER-IN-LAW is a Methodist minister in Memphis, Tennessee. He says that he will never forget the day that Martin Luther King Jr. was shot. Nor will he forget the day after, when a large group of clergy in Memphis decided to march to City Hall.

The clergy gathered at St. Mary's Episcopal Cathedral. At the last moment, the dean went into the cathedral and took the cross. Holding it high above him, he led the march down Poplar Avenue, down toward City Hall. The air was electric. Down the streets they marched.

There were many words spoken that day. But my father-in-law, to this day, still speaks about one sentence, one turn of phrase that he will never forget.

As the clergy were marching down Poplar Avenue, up ahead my father-in-law saw an elderly woman sitting on her front porch. As the procession approached her, she stood up and screamed, *"Get that cross back in the church where it belongs!"*

Joshua, son of Nun, must have sounded like that when he realized that Eldad and Medad, two Israelites, were prophesying outside of the tent. "My lord Moses, stop them!" he cried. Get that Spirit back in the tent where it belongs. People weren't supposed to be encountering God outside of the tent of meeting. They had put up this tent so that they would have an orderly, safe place to encounter God. And now Eldad and Medad were claiming that God's Spirit was resting on them in the camp. And what would come next? The dining room, in the kitchen . . . on the lawn?

And, in the Gospel, poor John rushes up to Jesus in a panic, all out of breath. "Teacher, we saw someone casting out demons in your name, and we tried to stop him, because he was not following us." He *wasn't* with us. He stepped out of the group by himself, in your name.

Stop them! Get that cross back into the church where it belongs! Get that Spirit back into the church where it belongs! Get those oracles back into the church where they belong! There should be no unpredictable, frightening encounters with God on these dirty streets. God's house is here, right here. We've set off a space for worship, a tent of meeting. Here we can encounter God once a week and then retreat to the safety of our secular lives. Isn't that what church is for?

I have a friend who lived and worked in Memphis years after my father-in-law marched down Poplar Avenue. Her name is Susan. Susan was the principal of a school in the city. In her years as principal, Susan met a woman who changed her understanding of where God could be encountered.

Susan met Guna on the first day of school. Guna was an elderly black woman on the janitorial staff. Susan said that no one cleaned like Guna. The bathrooms were immaculate. Susan thanked Guna for her work, and they got to talking. Guna was a Pentecostal Christian. She prayed all the time. And you could say that she prophesied. "Susan, you ain't going to stay here forever. You better start to pray about your future." "Susan, I think that child needs some extra attention." "Susan, now take some time for yourself, honey."

Soon they became friends. A black woman and a white woman. They even began to pray together. One day, Susan asked the question that had been bothering her a long time. "Guna, how do you do it? I mean, you clean toilets for a living. How do you keep so happy?"

And Guna answered with one simple sentence. "Honey, any job is a job for Jesus."

Guna stepped right out of her tent. She brought God with her even to the most menial tasks of her daily life. She found God on the streets, in the bathrooms, in the faces of children.

Are we afraid to follow Guna and step out of this tent? Are we, like Joshua or like that woman on the porch in Memphis, too afraid that things might get a bit out of control? Don't we believe that God waits for us out on the streets? Why are we afraid? Why are we afraid of Eldad and Medad? Why are we afraid of stepping out of this place?

You and I come here each week to be rejuvenated, to worship in a community. Yes, God is here—in the music that touches our souls, in the beauty, the majesty. It's all here to allow us to rest in God's presence. But then, every Sunday, we are sent out again. We are pushed out of the tent. To serve God out there. Yes, this is God's house. But God, God is not in here. No, God waits for us out *there*. Outside the tent. In the unpredictable, busy, messy lives that we lead.

Two weeks from now, the outreach committee will spend a Saturday morning stepping out into the neighborhood surrounding this church, and simply walking around. Everyone is invited. Our main purpose will be to ask ourselves, "What is out there? Where is God calling us to serve others in this neighborhood? What are the needs of this community?" And when we find out the answers to these questions, we hope to start addressing the needs of the community that surrounds this church. And we will ask you to join us.

Do you know what the names Eldad and Medad mean in Hebrew? "Beloved" and "Loved by God." Loved, and therefore bold enough to risk encountering God on the street, in the home, in their lives.

Let's get that cross out on the streets where it belongs! God waits for us, in the face of the child who doesn't have enough to eat, in the trust of a man who walks the streets, lost and confused. Come, meet, gather, worship in this place, and then go. Get out of here. Go in peace to love and serve the Lord.

Katherine B. Moorehead is Assistant to the Rector
at St. John's Church, West Hartford, Connecticut.

PROPER TWENTY-TWO

We Are the Possessions

Mark 10:17–31
Linda Wofford Hawkins

IT CAME TO ME the day we put together the swing set. It took five hours of concentration for me to read the directions aloud, line by line, while Mr. Fixit followed those directions. Then on the last page was the command to test the set for safety once a month. It suddenly occurred to me: If we did all the things we were supposed to do in order to care for all our possessions, that is all we would do in life. There would be time and attention for absolutely nothing else. I suddenly asked the question—who is serving whom? Are these material things here to serve me, or am I here to serve the swing set and the washing machine? At that moment, I felt truly captive to my possessions. I felt an urge toward freedom but could not imagine how to set myself free.

The man who goes down in history as the Rich Young Ruler was as captive to his possessions as we. He had everything that he could possibly want, the good life of the first century. He had obeyed the commandments all his life, yet something was missing. He did not feel satisfied. He felt a deep hunger for something more, so he came to Jesus asking that powerful question, "What must I do to inherit eternal life?"

Who is this man who stops Jesus on his journey? We often call him the Rich Young Ruler, although here in Mark he is neither "young" (as in the Gospel of Matthew), nor a "ruler" or elder of the synagogue (as he is in the Gospel of Luke). Here he is only "a man." In other words, he is just a person like any of us. Evidently he is a religious person who really tries to be faithful. Since his youth, he has kept all the commandments Jesus mentions. There is no reason to think he is self-righteous or evil. He is truly trying to do his very best as a person of God. As a faithful member of the household of God, he understands his wealth as a sign of God's favor, as a sign of his righteousness. He has all the things that give life meaning.

Jesus looks at him and loves him. This is the only time in the Synoptic Gospels that Jesus is said to love someone in particular. Clearly Jesus wants very much for him to become one of his own. He yearns for him to become who he was meant to be and follow him into the Kingdom of God.

Jesus invites the man to break out of his bondage and enter a new life of freedom. He speaks to him in the language of the possessions, which control his life. Jesus says, "You lack one thing; go, sell what you own, and give the money to the poor, and you will have treasure in heaven. . . ." Jesus can see that even as the man kneels before him he is looking for yet one more possession. He wants to know what to do to inherit eternal life. Eternal life is yet one more possession, the ultimate toy for the person who has everything. He is still preoccupied with himself and his own spirituality. Eternal life is something to get for himself. Jesus diagnoses his disease and offers his prescription for the cure. Give up all your possessions, all the things that possess you.

We can interpret the saying of Jesus in many ways. We can look at the things inside us that block us, the things we must set aside in order to give our all to Jesus. Indeed plenty of "things," as it were, in our lives can take the place of God. A few years ago I was convinced that our national preoccupation with health and fitness was becoming a new religion, an idol for our worship. Now I suspect that our preoccupation with spirituality runs the same danger.

All these preoccupations that put self in place of God do indeed stand as obstacles to our relationship with God, but we are missing something if we fail to hear the very specific message that Jesus is giving us. He really is saying something very specific about our material possessions. They show us most clearly how something else can take the place of God. After all, one-sixth of the quoted words of Jesus and one-third of the parables deal with money. Jesus fully appreciated the power of money. We can say we are not rich—that is somebody else. I am sure we all felt very rich Friday night when we heard about the church gathering where there was no bread and wine. Indeed in our world in comparison with our neighbors all over the globe, there are two definitions of wealth—first, a choice of what to eat today. And second, access to transportation. Guess what? All of us are wealthy.

Someone once observed that those who have *means* think the most important thing in life is *love*; the *poor*, however, know that what matters most in life is *money*. Indeed Jesus knew that money matters. He knew that we are material creatures in the midst of material reality. The things that we can see and feel get our attention. That swing set is pretty hard to ignore. Our possessions are more real than anything else. We may trust that this world of eternal life and treasure in heaven that Jesus describes does exist, but we know that the world of our material possessions exists for damn sure. We can print IN GOD WE TRUST on our coins, but we sure trust the feel of that money in our pockets.

The man in our story comes so close. He comes so close to accepting the invitation of Jesus to enter the abundant life. His story is a rare one in the gospels—the story of a person who says no to Jesus and grieves over his own decision. He wants to say yes, but he has many possessions and cannot take the leap. If he truly owned his own property, he could let go, but his possessions own *him*, and they will not let go. He is caught in a trap and cannot get out.

I am told that in India there is a traditional method used by hunters to trap monkeys. Half of a coconut shell is placed over some food that the monkey would want. A hole is carved in the shell just big enough for the hand to enter but not big enough for the hand to come out while grasping the food. The monkey comes along and goes straight for that food. It will hang on for dear life, clutching the food and trapping itself with its own unrelenting greed.

We human beings can be like that monkey. We hang on for dear life to the very thing that will be our undoing. We become trapped as we keep clutching the things that are given us. As we hold on so tight, we trap ourselves and give up our freedom to act, to move into the very abundant life that we desire.

Jesus knew well that we material people in our material world need to act. Therefore he gave the man a very specific set of instructions, action words meant to mobilize him—go, sell, give, come, follow. He needed to take action to become part of the Kingdom, part of the journey of Jesus. Jesus calls him to get up from his knees and get moving.

Yet the man says no. He trusts more in his possessions than in the promise of a new security in Christ. He is lulled into the self-sufficiency of the material. As he walks away, Jesus says, "How hard it will be for those who have wealth to enter the Kingdom of God!" Eugene Peterson's version says, "How difficult it is for people who have it all to enter the kingdom of God." Some of the manuscripts read, "How hard it is for those who trust in riches to enter the Kingdom of God!" Indeed *trusting* in those riches is what the issue is all about. The man could not relinquish his trust in riches long enough to pull his hand through that hole and put his hand in the hand of Jesus.

The disciples asked the question that is on our minds as well: "Then who can be saved?" None of us can make this leap alone. None of us. Jesus says, "For mortals it is impossible, but not for God; for God all things are possible." It is only by God's grace that precedes and follows us. Jesus invites us to open up to God's generosity. Open our hands to receive God's good gifts, and then open our hands to share them. Let go. Let God take over so there is nothing left of self. Let go. Relax and let God's grace flow over, around, and through us. For God, anything is possible.

We are the possessions. We are held in the hands of our possessions. Yet we are God's, *God's* creatures, *God's* possessions. May we then receive the grace that God gives, the grace that can open the trap and let us go free. May we grasp the hand of Jesus and join him in the journey into the Kingdom of God.

Linda Wofford Hawkins is Associate Rector at the Church of the Good Shepherd, Baltimore, Maryland.

PROPER TWENTY-EIGHT

The End Times

Daniel 12:1–13; Hebrews 10:31–39; Mark 13:14–23
Amanda Rutherford Ray

THE END TIMES are not something we think of often in the Episcopal Church. We are better at the parables, the prophecies, and the prayers than at the predictions of the end of the world. The readings today, however, focus our attention squarely on the teachings from both the Old Testament and the New Testament on the end times.

The book of Daniel provides the most memorable visions of the end times in the Old Testament. Daniel was written in the second century before the birth of Christ, about 164–167 B.C., when the Jews in Israel were being persecuted under the rule of Antiochus Epiphanes. The story of Daniel, however, is set at the time of the Babylonian king Nebuchadnezzar and the Persian kings Cyrus and Darius, in the mid-sixth century B.C.

Daniel, the hero of the book, was brought to the court of King Nebuchadnezzar as a captive from Jerusalem. The first of the stories of Daniel really involved his three friends Shadrach, Meshach, and Abednego, whom you probably remember from Sunday school as the three young men thrown in the fiery furnace who were saved by God because of their faith. The story continued with Daniel interpreting dreams, much like Joseph before him, for the kings of Babylon and Persia. Daniel interpreted the "handwriting on the wall" and eventually survived being thrown into the lion's den. All these stories are told to exemplify Daniel's faithfulness to God, even in the worst of times.

Our reading this morning focuses on Daniel's vision of the end times. Daniel, standing by the Tigris River, saw the angel Gabriel. The angel spoke to Daniel of the succession of kings on earth, from the time of the story (the sixth century) to the time of the author (the second century), and of the battles of the angels in heaven representing each of the nations, culminating in a great tribulation that precedes the end of time. On that final day, the people of Israel who still lived would be delivered from their oppressors, and many of the dead would be raised—some to everlasting life and some to everlasting contempt.

Interestingly, it was to this passage from Daniel that Jesus referred as he walked out of the temple with his disciples. The disciples were admiring the building, impressed by the large stones—said to be thirty-seven feet long, eighteen feet wide and twelve feet thick—massive and permanent. And Jesus responded to them by prophesying that "not one stone will be left upon another; all will be thrown down." He spoke of the "desolating sacrilege," language from Daniel referring to the pagan statues that would be set up in the temple by the

Romans, as the sign of the end. Sometime after these signs, a time of suffering would be followed by a time when all creation would be dark:

> *. . . The sun will be darkened,*
> *and the moon will not give its light,*
> *and the stars will be falling from heaven,*
> *and the powers in the heavens will be shaken.*

And finally Jesus promised his return:

> *Then they will see the 'Son of Man coming in clouds'* [again language from Daniel] *with great power and glory. Then he will send out the angels, and gather his elect from the four winds, from the ends of the earth to the ends of heaven.*

It is one of those times in the Gospels when we see Jesus speaking with certainty of judgment and the end of the world. But even then, he said to his disciples,

> *But about that day or hour no one knows, neither the angels in heaven, nor the Son, but only the Father. Beware, keep alert; for you do not know when the time will come. . . . And what I say to you I say to all: Keep awake."* [1]

We, of course, are not those who believe that we can predict the end of the world. If questioned closely, many of us would find it difficult even to imagine God ending the world. It doesn't fit with our picture of ourselves—in charge. If we worry about the end of the world at all, it is concern over weapons of mass destruction. But the return of Christ at the end of time, like the Resurrection, is a tenet of our faith. In the Nicene Creed we can read the words, "He will come again in glory to judge the living and the dead and his Kingdom will have no end." And in the Eucharistic prayers, we say, "We await his coming in glory." And in the Lord's Prayer, we say, "Thy Kingdom come . . . on earth as it is in heaven." All statements reflecting our belief as a church that Christ will come again in glory at the end of the age. But what does that promise mean for us today?

I have had the privilege for the last three years of serving as the executive director of Episcopal Community Services. This agency provides services in San Diego and Riverside counties: low-cost family counseling, early childhood education, adult literacy, chaplaincy services to juvenile offenders, a foster family agency for children hardest to place, drug and alcohol rehabilitation and education, HIV testing and counseling, services to battered women and children, emergency assistance, housing and employment for the homeless, services and shelter for the mentally ill, employment programs for those making the transition from welfare to work, and chaplaincy services to all our programs.

She came to our Safe Havens program in Oceanside, having been homeless for two years, weighing eighty-five pounds. She was young, only twenty-six. She heard voices—voices in her head telling her she was ugly and fat—that her food was poisoned—that people were trying to kill her.

The name of her problem was psychotic anorexia nervosa. Her name was Amy. She paced the floors talking to herself and no one else. She wouldn't eat—afraid of being poisoned. After two weeks our staff began to see some progress. Amy decided to talk and agreed to go to County Mental Health as an outpatient, as long as she could come back to Safe Havens. The doctor prescribed antipsychotics, and with the support of her friends at the house, she stayed on the medication and began to eat. After some months she made contact with her family and is now living with them again in Arizona. Safe Havens is a program to bring the severely mentally ill and chronically homeless into a safe environment where they can begin to recover from living on the streets and eventually find stable housing.

Amy's mother wrote me a letter after her daughter had returned home, part of which I would like to share with you:

> Only seven months ago, I had given up any hope of ever seeing my daughter alive again. In late 1993 she had a breakdown triggered by the use of drugs, terminated her professional employment, and was on the streets of San Diego in a state of confusion and paranoia. Despite family efforts to intervene . . . she fell through the cracks and lived as homeless and missing until September 1996, when I received a call from a county homeless outreach worker stating she had possibly been located and identified. This began a six-month period of well-designed services that allowed Amy to stabilize, begin recovery, and reconnect with her family.
>
> Amy is making the transition from the Safe Havens Project now to more independent living. . . . Her long term goal is to return to employment, and I am sure she will be able to do this. All of this is a dream coming true for Amy's family, and we want to acknowledge Episcopal Community Services and all who support it for saving a very precious life.

For Amy's family the end of the world didn't come through the weapons of mass destruction, but through drugs of choice. Darkness overcame them, not because the sun ceased to shine or the moon failed to provide light, but because a much loved child, who desperately needed help, disappeared. Although we wait for Christ's coming in glory, the end of the world sometimes comes for us in addiction, abuse, sickness, and suffering.

What does the promise of Christ's coming in glory mean for us today? I believe that it is the basis of our hope for the future. Although we may not face in our lifetimes the end of the world as we know it—we will certainly face our own death and that of those we love. And some of us will face great suffering. The book of Daniel speaks of the faithful being purified, cleansed, and refined, the author of Hebrews of abuse and persecution, and Jesus of martyrdom. It is not easy to be a Christian.

But the promise of the Gospels is the promise of the Resurrection and the promise of the return of Christ in glory. The promise of love triumphing over evil—the promise of faithfulness conquering indifference—the promise of joy overcoming despair. In our work at ECS we see people every day who are suffering—abused, addicted, alienated, poor, sick, outcast—without hope and without help. But we believe that God speaks in these visions of the end times of hope and healing and redemption. And we believe that our call is to be faithful. To live each day as if it is our last. Not in indolence and defeat, but rather with joy and hope, looking forward to that time when we "see God face to face." As the author of the letter to the Hebrews reminds us:

". . . In a very little while, the one who is coming will come and will not delay; but my righteous one will live by faith. My soul takes no pleasure in anyone who shrinks back." But we are not among those who shrink back and so are lost, but among those who have faith and so are saved.[2]

Amanda Rutherford Ray is Executive Director of Episcopal Community Services, San Diego, California.

---

1. Mark 13:24–37.
2. Hebrews 10:37–39.

THANKSGIVING DAY

Spreading the Cloth at the Table of Thanks

Deuteronomy 8:1–10
Margaret A. Gat

TONIGHT I want to share something personal with you all. This is my grandmother's tablecloth. It *is* a bit seedy, and may not have much meaning for you. But as we all gather to celebrate the holidays with family and friends, we bring with us the richness and variety of our heritage. Everyone here shares in common some traditions of this holiday. We give thanks for the land and the freedom we know.

Everyone here shares different traditions, particular to who we are. As we gather together this evening, all, or most of us, are believers in the presence of God in our lives. That common thread would seem to be what binds us together. But sometimes I think that it is our individuality that makes us precious to God, and therefore to each other. We give thanks for who we are, and for what we share with each other and with God. For what God made is *good*.

And so I share with you the individuality of my grandmother's tablecloth.

Once upon a time, my grandmother lived on an island off the coast of Maine. In the summer it was a wonderful place to hang out the wash and let the fresh ocean breezes dry the clothes in a wink of an eye. The sheets and towels would wave in the breeze like soft puffy clouds against the deep blue of the ocean and the clear, bright sky.

Shortly before my mother's wedding, on just such a day, my Grandma decided to wash the good tablecloth. So she got out the washtub and went to work. When she was done, she took it outside and started to hang it. Before she could stick a single clothespin on it, one of those breezes raced along and snatched the tablecloth right off the line, and swept it into the sea. They say Grandma was beside herself, she was so upset. But there you are. The tablecloth was gone.

Each of us has been on a journey during the past year, each of us on our own path. Some of us have traveled through desert places where we have been sorely tested, but here we are. Most of us have known doubt. We have been unsure of ourselves, of our families, of God, or of each other at one time or another. Some of us have suffered loss, and know pain and anxiety. Sometimes the simple act of preparing for tomorrow's journey has seemed impossible. But we have continued, despite all those things that have held us back and made our travel difficult. So, we are here, tonight.

A couple of years later while Grandma was having her morning coffee, a local fisherman happened along. Old Capt'n Newell knocked on the door, calling out, "Good morning, Anna, I have something that I believe is yours." And he held up a soggy, seaweed-covered, dripping mess. "I caught this on my line this mornin'." Sure enough, Grandma got her tablecloth back.

The good fortune of the returned tablecloth captured the imagination of our island people. The story has been told and retold for several generations now. It is part of who we are, tattered and torn, no longer fresh and pristine, but very real.

Tonight we remember the old stories about God's people, told and retold for generations, when families have gathered to offer thanks for God's blessings. The stories are important to us; for they hold us together and bring meaning into our lives. There have been times when we have lost the old stories. Maybe they have lost meaning for us. Maybe there was no one left to tell us the story, or nobody to listen. Or maybe we could not hear the story as ours, because it was told so differently than what we remember. Change can be difficult. When things are not as we want them to be we can become lost and wander away. Sometimes we are ungrateful and angry, so we reject that which has had meaning for us.

Grandma looked with amazement at the sodden material. They say she first thought she should just put that mess right straight onto the dump. After some thought, she again got out the washtub and went to work. She washed it, and she washed it, and then laid the tablecloth on the grass to dry; for it is said, at least in my family folklore, that grass bleaches stains out of white cloth.

Someone said to me recently that, after years of looking down and seeing one problem after another at his feet, he had finally decided he could not continue to live that way, and so he made the simple decision to do something about it. Thus, he began to look up. He discovered hope and hard work waiting for him. He is grateful, for he also realized God's presence watching over him. And he was content to wait for the moment when he would discover God anew.

Grandma discovered a new tablecloth. It was not like anything she had known before, but it was still her best tablecloth. Its color was—interesting. Its story became part of its aura, but it had a new life. That new life has been passed down in our family ever since.

As we hear the old stories that are part of our Thanksgiving tradition, we incorporate them into the reality that we are today. We are no longer an isolated people, struggling to survive the winter in unheated hovels, eating whatever we can to keep us alive. But those ancestors are part of our memory, and they call us to give thanks for what we have, and to remember those who still struggle to survive. And when we reflect on our stories we know that there are divine forces that sustain us and encourage us. We know, because we can hear it in the stories about our ancestors. We can give thanks with confidence for who we are and what we have today.

We begin with our knowledge of the presence of God, and give thanks. Then we can set the table and prepare for the feast. We spread the tablecloth. It enriches our lives. Its story has become part of our story. It is not the tablecloth itself, it is the spirit of those that are part of its story that encourages me and guides me into a new life for tomorrow.

This tablecloth has become a symbol of my roots and my strength. It has no value, however, unless it is used as a symbol of hospitality for tomorrow. When we can set the table, knowing our heritage and the importance of sharing who we are and what we have with a stranger, and with those whom we love, our lives become richer.

This cloth will become the foundation for a much larger story of the presence of God, our advocate in the wilderness, who invites us to share what we have with those who are still lost. On our table we put the fruit of our labor, the bread that will sustain us, so that we can share our food, our joy, and our laughter with those we love and with those who are in need of our caring.

Yes, we come before the Lord with joy and thanksgiving, sharing song, story, laughter, and the love of God. We have each journeyed many miles this past year. It is right that we give thanks to God, as did Moses' people, for bringing us out of exile and offering us the many blessings that we receive, for the food, for this community and its suburbs, for the opportunity to worship with other people in this holy space.

Each of our families has its own special way of giving thanks, but all of our families share the tradition of Scripture. Tomorrow we shall eat and talk and share our spirit and our food. Tonight let us give thanks, according to our common tradition, in the same way that God's children have offered their thanks for thousands of years.

It is written, "You shall eat your fill and bless the Lord your God for the good land that he has given you."

וְאָכַלְתָּ וְשָׂבָעְתָּ וּבֵרַכְתָּ אֶת־יְהוָה אֱלֹהֶיךָ עַל־הָאָרֶץ הַטֹּבָה אֲשֶׁר נָתַן־לָךְ:

AMEN

My thanks to Cantor Jack Korbman of Adoth Shalom Synagogue for his assistance with the Hebrew text.

Margaret A. Gat is Priest-in-Charge of
St. John's Church, Dover, New Jersey.

■ 5

THE PREACHER AS THEOLOGIAN AND TEACHER

Judith M. McDaniel

AT A RECENT meeting of the College for Bishops, two friends were chatting during a coffee break. The newly consecrated bishop said, "I was so relieved to learn from the lecture by the Dean of X Seminary yesterday that a bishop no longer needs to be a theologian." "We-e-ll, I didn't hear that lecture," said his friend, "but I don't think I agree with him." Replied the new bishop, "Oh, he just meant that we don't have to be constituting theology, like the early bishops." "What, then," said his friend, "do you think you're doing when you're preaching?"

What do you and I think we are doing when we're preaching? We know some things we are *not* doing. We are not delivering a written essay on its hind legs. We're not lecturing. We're not sharing historical-critical methodology or displaying our exegetical expertise. We aren't moralizing. But what do you and I think we're doing when we're preaching if it is not creating, forming, and teaching theology? What was Paul doing when he wrote his letters to the newly forged churches of the New Testament if it wasn't creating theology as he went along? Whose god will fill the void if you and I do not speak theologically?

To have any meaningful conversation about the preacher as theologian and teacher in today's church, you and I need first to examine the theological presuppositions we hold about Anglican homiletical theory and practice. We need to be conscious of the premises on which we stake our claims for proclamation.

Judging by the preaching I have heard for the past twenty-five years, I venture that the majority of Anglicans are incarnational in homiletical theory and practice. Our sacramental emphasis locates the Word of God in human experience and creation. The question at issue, however, is How do we arrive at that incarnational center? Where is our point of beginning?

In a recent article entitled "Theological Method and Episcopal Vocation," an American bishop wrote of his denomination, "Anglicans . . . tend to do theology from 'below to above,' from experience to concept to truth [and, finally,] to action."[1] He continued, "In theology our reflection on our *experience* of God does not constitute a fourth source of authority *per se*, but is [*sic*] *a priori* upon which the Scripture, tradition and reason are dependent." In other words, this author privileges experience before Scripture, tradition, or reason. In his article he uses experience forty-four times as the ground for judgment of all things meaningful theologically.

There is something about this analysis that reminds me of Barth's comment about Schleiermacher. You remember. Barth claimed that what Schleiermacher really wanted to do was to speak about God by "speaking of man in a loud voice." I would certainly agree that God is *available* to us in our experience. At the very least, the doctrines of creation and incarnation compel us to affirm that God believed the created world to be good and, at a moment in time, was moved to empty himself and all goodness for it.[2] God is surely present *to* our experience, but is God present *in* our experience? The question of the direction of incarnational flow has led some experiential-expressivists[3] to argue, with Bultmann, that creation and redemption are one. A Bultmannian incarnational preacher begins with humankind, and humankind's experience.

On the other hand, one who reads Anselm would define incarnational theology as the union of humankind with the *person*, but *not* with the *nature* of God. That is, an individual may be in relationship with God, but no individual can contain God's fullness. Therefore, an Anselmian preacher would be more prone to begin with the Word of God as found in the biblical witness, rather than to begin with human experience.

But even beginning with the biblical text has its problems. We look at the text from a perspective. Modern hermeneutical theory implicitly recognizes the possibility of several interpretations of a single text. In part that is because numerous messages can be derived from a single text. Furthermore, several interpretations of a single text are possible, because there is no such thing as an unbiased stance from which to do exegesis, no such thing as an objective perspective. Each of us has a horizon from which we view the world; and that amalgam of experience and education influences what we see. We approach Scripture constrained by the cultural patterns or context of our upbringing. Our understanding of Scripture is not pure, because our epistemology, our very way of knowing, is culturally conditioned. Each of us has an interpretive stance, a bias from which we exegete texts. The hermeneutical stance we take toward a biblical text determines the method we use to exegete that text; and the method we select predetermines what we will discover. "Method, understood as a preestablished set of procedures for investigating some phenomenon, in fact not only attains its object but creates its object."[4]

If only since the publication of Gadamer's *Truth and Method*,[5] most preachers have been willing to admit that there is no such thing as an unbiased stance from which to interpret Scripture. As the aforementioned bishop wrote, "We engage the text within a given context or historical/cultural situation which shapes our appropriation and interpretation of how and what we express. . . ."[6] In other words, we have to begin where we are.

But to privilege our own experience as the place in which the gospel comes to life is dangerous. Humankind and humankind's experience are not identical to divine revelation and inspiration.

The Bible is a witness to God. It is a record of a people's response to God's self-revelation, and of their subsequent inspiration. Certainly God is larger than the biblical writers' understandings; but, likewise, God is larger than our own capacities for understanding. If much of our preaching is approached from an incarnational, sacramental hermeneutical stance, the inherent risk is that we will privilege our personal experience over the biblical story, and substitute anthropology for theology. And who among us wants any part of a Savior who is nothing more than a projection of our own needs?

The tension between these two stories—the theological and the anthropological—has been with us for a long time. For generations the incarnational flow of preaching was deductive, the "three points and a poem" model. The preacher extracted from the text an idea. From this abstract proposition, the preacher then established three points by which he hoped to demonstrate application to human life. The deductive model is a teaching vehicle; and heaven knows, in our biblically illiterate culture, we need to teach. But the weakness of this cognitive-propositional approach is that too often the proclamation of the gospel remains an external ideal, an unattainable moralism. And in the middle of this century, homiletics, right along with the rest of social consciousness, reached a crisis.

In response, liberal theology reversed the direction of homiletical practice. Inductive preaching rejected abstract propositions in favor of experiential knowledge. Inductive sermons begin with a particular experience, then move to a universal principle. In the sermon, an event of self-recognition becomes the icon. What the listeners *feel* becomes the measure of received knowledge, rather than what is learned intellectually.

Obviously, the antitheses between the deductive and the inductive models of preaching can be too starkly drawn. Saying that one approach is all "head" and the other all "heart" does not do justice to the complexities of communication. But the two trajectories are clear. The deductive approach at its worst is a mere *description of belief*; the inductive, *a simplistic explanation of how to believe*. Neither can be equated with kerygmatic proclamation.

As bearers of the tradition, ordained preachers often find themselves caught in the tension between theology and anthropology, caught between *guarding* versus boldly *proclaiming* an interpretation of the core story into differing circumstances, struggling to hold to the incarnational center of kerygmatic proclamation. That struggle is nothing new. It was Jesus' struggle as well.

Jesus evoked wonder by the power of his words. He invited others to be his messengers, provided them with a message, and gave them the power to deliver it. The incarnational flow of his message, however, was consistently detoured. The message was delivered but diverted, and he constantly had to regroup.

Those he summoned were called to preach, to teach the message of a radically different reality, and to make judgment and repentance possible. What, then, did they do? Rather than proclaiming, "Your sins are forgiven," they preferred, "Pick up your stretcher and walk." Oh, the disciples were given authority to cast out demons, but they mistook the purpose of that power. They brought to Jesus demoniacs, lepers, paralytics. These he *did* heal; but these miracles were symbolic actions. Healing was not and is not an end in itself. Healing is not the essential word. Rather, self-discernment, judgment, metanoia is the end.

The disciples, however, didn't get it. *Ministry* threatened to overtake the *message*. It was not ministry that was Jesus' concern. It was the message. So Jesus regrouped. He withdrew, and again and again called disciples to be with him, and to go forth preaching.

Ministry has become our concern as well, to the detriment of the message. So consumed with delivery of aid that we have made substance secondary, we, the church, are in danger of becoming indistinguishable from any other social service agency. Even worse, instead of inviting people to hear a message that evokes wonder, and providing them with the tools to spread that message, the church expends enormous resources of time and energy screening the message bearers. Like the early disciples, modern message bearers adopt a therapeutic model of ministry. They promote health. Healthy psyches, healthy habits, healthy families, and healthy bank accounts make healthy churches.

And all the while an echo whispers in our hearing. We are not called to heal one another. God alone heals. We are called to proclaim a message, to lead people to hear the Word of Good News and to turn toward it. Without that message as the beginning and end of our witness, we will be children of a lesser god.

Jesus' message is not meant for people with plenty of health—as determined by Commissions on Ministry, plenty of knowledge—as assessed by General Ordination Exams, plenty of security—as certified by diplomas. His text is meant for people of passion. The only criterion for bearing his message is hearing.

Jesus' message is not meant to comfort you or me. It is meant to change us. The only standard of judgment is repentance. Jesus' message is not meant to provide answers for the way we live our lives. It is meant to call into question the very grounds on which we stand. The only principle is the message: Jesus is the beginning and the end. Jesus is the Word of the Lord.

What, then, is kerygmatic proclamation? It is stating, with Anselm, "I believe in order to understand. I believe in order to perceive. I believe in order to reorient my life." Kerygmatic proclamation is epistemology. It is a way of knowing. It is language that shapes experience. Kerygmatic proclamation tells us *how* we know *what* we know, as well as the *content* of that knowing. If you doubt that language shapes experience or, as Heidegger said, "Language precedes experience," think for a moment of the scene in *The Miracle Worker*. Annie Sullivan holds Helen Keller's hand under the water cascading from the outdoor pump, all the while spelling the word water into Helen's outstretched palm. Until Helen Keller had a word for the sensation she was experiencing, she had no world.

Only God creates with the Word, but the preacher's words have the power to name the world as *what* it is and *whose* it is. To preach kerygmatically is to preach Jesus. It is to proclaim that God's world is the only reality; and that the world, as many know it, is to be incorporated into God's perspective, not vice versa. The Sunday bulletin at St. Andrew's Cathedral (Jackson, Mississippi)[7] puts it this way: "It is the continued presence of the Holy Spirit which incorporates our lives into the risen life of Christ, and makes us part of his body." In other words, we are to be incorporated into the biblical story, and that incorporation is a continuing process.

Preaching is always eschatological, never finished. We tell the story, not attempting to reconcile the Jesus of history with the Christ of faith as if to ask, "What did he know and when did he know it?" No, we tell the whole biblical story, whose revelatory logic and content lead us to the identity of the man known as Jesus of Nazareth, and lead us to become one with the Christ.

But is just telling the story enough? Erich Auerbach's important book *Mimesis*[8] demonstrates the power of the genre "narrative" to make a claim on our lives. Drawing on Auerbach, Hans Frei—who is closely associated with the narrative theology movement—cites four important characteristics of "realistic narrative"[9]: First, the narrative's shape, including its chronological sequence, is critical to its meaning. Second, character and circumstance cannot be rendered separately. Third, realistic narrative is "history-like." And finally, the sublime constantly mixes with the ordinary. When we listen deeply to the biblical story, we are listening not simply to the Word in Scripture, but to the word at the heart of our own lives as well. So how might you and I tell the biblical story in a way that enables listeners to listen deeply and become incorporated into Scripture's story?

The biblical story is completed with a vision of the heavenly city. It concludes with the promise that "those who are written in the . . . book of life . . . will see the face of God and will reign with God and his Christ forever and ever."[10] Incredible, isn't it? How far from our earthly cities is this vision of well-being and joy! How far from our experience! Much of the Bible's vision is a symbolic appeal to our imaginations, but one thing at least is clear. This is the story of the ultimate triumph of God's goodness over the evils of the present, a reversal of this world's order. As such, it is a narrative of the dissonance between the way things are and the way things ought to be. It causes us to ponder, "Must discord and destruction dominate life on earth; or is there some other way we should interpret this story for the present age?" It is like shouting into the wind to cry, "Show me a new vision. Tell me a new story." And so we turn to one another and ask, "Tell me . . . your story."

If someone were to ask you that question—tell me your story—what would you say? All of us have been asked, "Where do you go to school?" Or, "What do you do, vocationally?" Or, "What keeps you busy?" All of those questions—whether at coffee hour after church, or at casual gatherings from Boston to San Diego, Seattle to Palm Beach—all are gracious attempts to say, "Tell me something about yourself."

But, "Tell me your story"? That's a different kind of question. That question is ordinarily posed when a reflective response is expected. Often we are called upon to answer that question at moments of decision, when we are charting new directions for our lives. "Tell me your story" elicits an autobiographical parable. It requires redescription, not explanation. "Tell me your story" asks us to interpret our lives. But do we really understand what that kind of interpretation means?

At an ecumenical conference of preachers last summer in Kyoto, Japan, there were professors in attendance from eighteen different countries. Not all spoke

English, so it was necessary to have on hand two simultaneous translators. But the Japanese did not call our language experts "translators." They called them, more accurately, "interpreters"; for what they were doing was redescribing reality. Moving from one language to another requires a redescription of reality. It requires moving from one thought world to another, one culture to another, one context to another. Never has it been clearer to me than in Japan that language shapes, and even precedes, experience. For the first time in my life I preached a forty-five minute sermon because it took that long to interpret fifteen minutes of English into Japanese categories of thought. Interpretation reconfigures reality.

How do you and I interpret our lives? What is the story we tell ourselves about ourselves? If we frame our story in terms of our job history, that will probably mean leaving out our childhood and some of our most formative years. If we tell our story in terms of our accomplishments, that may mean omitting some of our most important relationships. How do we frame our story? What stance do we take when we begin interpreting our lives?

In the stories we read in the Bible, prophets, priests, and kings sketch an interpretation of life, life then and life now. They move us from one thought world to another, framing all of life's story in the Bible's story. They remind us that each of our lives' stories is incorporated in the Bible's redescription of reality. They tell us our life stories begin and end in the Bible's proclamations and promises.

Take the story of Paul's healing of the lame man in Lystra, for instance. Paul sees that the man had faith to be healed, and he is healed. The lame man's faith translates his life from one realm into another. The miracle occurs not on the basis of the man's potential or Paul's intrinsic good will. No, the miracle occurs on the basis of God's conception of the future, a future of wholeness, of *shalom*. Healthy faith causes the man to stand up for what he believes, and his life is reconfigured. With the perspective of faith, the lame man envisions a new reality, redescribing and reinterpreting the life he once knew, incorporating it into a new Being. Most miraculous of all, this glimpse of God's future occurs outside the boundaries of the established order, outside the protective walls of the synagogue, outside the sheltered community of Christian worship.

And what is Paul's proclamation in that setting? What is Paul's interpretation of this event? He preaches his first sermon to a pagan audience by redescribing their reality, giving them new categories in which to think about life: "Turn to the living God," he says, "the One who made the heaven and the earth and the sea and all that is in them. . . . He has not left himself without a witness to goodness—giving you rains from heaven and fruitful seasons, and filling you with food and your hearts with joy."[11] Paul is not trying to make the creation story from Genesis relevant to current cultural trends. He is readjusting the vision of the pagans to see the world from the Bible's perspective. He is pulling them into the biblical story. He is making the Bible's reality their reality.

If Paul, the earliest author in the New Testament, stands outside civilization's establishments to tell us of our beginnings, the last author, the poet of

Revelation, fairly pole-vaults over the known world to tell us our end. "I saw no temple in the city, for its temple is the Lord God the Almighty. . . . And there will be no more night; they need no light of lamp or sun, for the Lord God will be their light."[12] Here is proclamation and promise, a promise that transcends our tangible, immediate, observable, personal experience.

Our experience is that the world offers us a dwelling in which evil more and more triumphs over good, a dwelling in which cruelty conquers kindness, a dwelling in which injustice reigns over righteousness. Interpret that reality. Is this situation simply to be accepted as the status quo? How would you describe it? Does it look like the capital of darkness? A city so full of corrupt practices that disgrace is a common headline in the daily papers? A city so lacking in civility that slander is everyday parlance? A city so wanting in community that the rich segregate themselves in enclaves for protection against the poor? A city in which neighbors cannot be trusted? A city in which children kill other children daily? That is the language of our experience. That is the interpretation of anguish.

Is it any wonder in such a city that parents are so uncertain of their own values they dare not attempt to pass them on to their young? That we have spawned a generation that never had any faith to begin with, and so have no faith to lose? Should it be a surprise that in such a hedonistic miasma "desire [is] quickly elevated to the level of need and then [those] alleged needs are further elevated to. . . rights"?[13] It cannot be a coincidence that the books on our shelves by the interpreters of American society have such titles as *The Culture of Disbelief*[14] and *Life after God*.[15]

It has been said ad nauseam that we are now living in the post-Christendom era, and we all know the two prominent professors of theology at Duke Divinity School who have written that Christians must now consider themselves *Resident Aliens*.[16] Are you satisfied with that description, or is there something new for you and me to preach?

This country and this world desperately need a redescription of reality. If we do not find a new way to interpret which hungers are worth having, we will starve to death. Our book of life, the Bible, never . . . ever provides any *explanation* for the reality of evil in this world. The biblical story does not explain reality. It *redescribes* reality. It tells us the way things are in God's eyes and invites us to adjust our vision to see the world from the Bible's perspective.

If the preacher has a theological responsibility, hidden in that claim is the fact that the preacher also has a teaching responsibility. A teaching responsibility does not mean that the sermon distances itself from experiential depth to become an abstract, sterile lecture. It means that we approach our point of incarnational beginning to ask ourselves not only what the text is saying but also what the text is doing. By asking what the text is saying, we are inquiring about its content. But asking what the text is doing is equally important. When we ask what the text is doing, we are looking for patterns of meaning. Patterns are the narrative shape critical to meaning to which Hans Frei referred. What the text is doing is its rhetorical strategy; and strategy is conveyed by form. Form carries a text of its own, apart from the lexical meaning of the words;[17] and form impacts the total meaning apprehended.

Form or agency is revelatory. A preacher who is theologian and teacher needs a storehouse of evocative forms. Often, form conveys the affective element of a pericope or a sermon. This is not to say that the content of words does not convey feeling; but form can convey emotion at a subliminal level.

Think for a moment of the arrangement of syllables to achieve assonance[18] or consonance [19] in a poem and how that repetition moves the listener along in a rhythmical pulse. Similarly, in prose individual words, in addition to syllables, contain both affective and cognitive components that can be arranged in rhythmical patterns for impact. As Kenneth Burke put it:

> Form *in [prose] is an arousing and fulfillment of desires. A work has form insofar as one part of it leads a [listener] to anticipate another part, to be gratified by the sequence.*[20]

Notice how much more memorable Burke's own statement is if its form is paraphrased in an ancient rhetorical pattern used by Augustine, Ambrose, and Jerome to read: *Form is the creation of an expectation and its subsequent satisfaction.*

So we approach the biblical text looking for and analyzing both content and form, both what the text is saying and what the text is doing. What the text is doing is a question of information management or process. The process question asks what the text hopes to accomplish and how it proposes to do so. It isn't so much concerned with our intellectual assent as it is with our heartfelt response.

In his introduction to the *Confessions*, translator Henry Chadwick characterizes the rhetoric of Augustine's writing as layered with "harmonics of deeper meaning."[21] By this description Chadwick means that the structure of Augustine's sentences and clauses—and sometimes even his choice of words as signs—imparts significance and makes cognitive connections that cannot be indicated by literal speech. Much like chords of music, the form of Augustine's word choice and placement conveys overtones of meaning. By this means Augustine's rhetoric reached a complex inner and external world then and indicates how preachers might penetrate a complex inner and external world now. That classical, Christian rhetorician brought to expression intuitive understandings that are difficult to verbalize; and in doing so, he managed to communicate something ineffable.

Rhetorical strategy is a process of discovery, a process of identifying, associating, and binding ideas in patterns that of themselves convey meaning. Pattern or structure carries a text of its own. The correspondence of wisdom and eloquence conveys more meaning than straightforward statements of fact. Harmonics of deeper meaning come via information management, and preachers utilize harmonics and make connections by intentionally focusing on the process of linking words with words, signs with signs. Concentrating on the process of how language works can enhance the management of a preacher's special information and his or her capacity for getting something heard, but it can also create new understanding.

Preaching is involved in the process of knowing. But process itself is cognitive, it makes connections that were not previously made; so preaching has the potential to create new knowledge, new understanding. In the process of linking thoughts to words, preaching is creative of a new reality. The *content* of what is revealed is significant. But the *way* thoughts are connected is also meaningful. Because meaning is at the core of human experience, reality redescribed and newly perceived is experienced as a genuinely new reality. Incarnational preaching that evokes a reality absorbed into the world of the biblical story will feed people not a blue plate special, but a heavenly banquet in which the bread of the Word is broken and shared.

So tell the Christian story, preacher. Revision this world. Interpret your future to reconfigure it in God's terms. You have a Savior who was flung down and nailed up by just such a people who thought they were in charge of the world, people of status, power, influence, wealth who thought they were in charge of their lives. Tell the story of the cross, Christian, the story of the tree of life whose leaves are for the healing of the nations, for what we need to heal us is something beyond the political, something beyond the economic. We need something of the Spirit.[22] Find a way to tell the world your story, Christian, the story of a cross, of a broken, crucified, self-giving people who are bound to triumph in God's *shalom*. Tell the world the Christian story, preacher. Share with the world the Christian perception of reality. Redescribe reality in Christian terms for the rest of humanity. Interpret your beginning and your end. We need it, now.

*Judith M. McDaniel is Associate Professor of Homiletics
at Virginia Theological Seminary, Alexandria, Virginia.*

---

1. Craig B. Anderson, "Theological Method and Episcopal Vocation," *Anglican Theological Review* (LXXVII:1):31–46.

2. "For our sake he made him to be sin who knew no sin, so that in him we might become the righteousness of God" (2 Corinthians 5:21).

3. George A. Lindbeck, *The Nature of Doctrine: Religion and Theology in a Postliberal Age* (Philadelphia: Westminster Press, 1984), 16.

4. Sandra M. Schneiders, *The Revelatory Text: Interpreting the New Testatment as Sacred Scripture* (San Francisco: Harper, 1991), 23.

5. Hans-Georg Gadamer, *Truth and Method,* second rev. ed., trans. Joel Weinsheimer and Donald G. Marshall (New York: Crossroad, 1989).

6. Anderson, 32.

7. Quoting from "The People's Work."

8. Erich Auerbach, *Mimesis: The Representation of Reality in Western Literature,* trans. Willard R. Trask (Princeton: Princeton University Press, 1953).

9. Charles L. Campbell, *Preaching Jesus: New Directions for Homiletics in Hans Frei's Postliberal Theology* (Grand Rapids: William B. Eerdmans, 1997), 16, n. 440.

10. Revelation 21:22–22:7.

11. Acts 14:15, 17.

12. Revelation 21:22, 25b, 23.

13. William H. Willimon, "Hunger in This Abandoned Generation," in *Sharing Heaven's Music: The Heart of Christian Preaching*, ed. Barry L. Callen (Nashville: Abingdon Press, 1995), 31.

14. Stephen L. Carter, *The Culture of Disbelief: How American Law and Politics Trivialize Religious Devotion* (New York: BasicBooks, 1993).

15. Douglas Coupland, *Life After God* (New York: Pocket Books, 1997).

16. Stanley Hauerwas and William H. Willimon, *Resident Aliens: Life in the Christian Colony* (Nashville: Abingdon Press, 1989).

17. For elaboration see Judith M. McDaniel, "Rhetoric Reconsidered: Preaching as Persuasion," *Sewanee Theological Review* 41:3 (1998): 241–252.

18. Repetition of vowels without repetition of consonants: so/bow/dough.

19. Repetition of consonants especially at end of stressed syllables without correspondence of vowels: dead/pride.

20. Kenneth Burke, *Counter-statement* (Berkeley: University of California Press, 1968), 124.

21. Augustine, *Confessions,* tr. Henry Chadwick (Oxford: Oxford University Press, 1991), ix.

22. Willimon, 30.

Preaching as Vigil, Feast, and Octave

Exodus 19:3–8a; 1 Peter 2:4–10
Roger Alling

WELCOME to the vigil for Pentecost; and welcome to the Preaching Excellence Program. It is appropriate that we gather on the eve of one of the church's great celebrations. A word about vigils, and what follows them, is in order.

Feasts follow vigils, and octaves and seasons follow feasts. The vigil is to the feast as Advent is to Christmas, and as Lent is to Easter.

We prepare in the vigil, celebrate on the feast, and reflect during the octave. If we're not prepared, the feasts have no impact. If the feasts have no impact, they make no lasting impression on our lives.

Vigils, feasts, and octaves are our way of organizing anticipation, culmination, and reflection. Because anticipation is a crucial part of this process, vigils are important.

Did you know that there is such a thing as a homiletical vigil? Let me tell you when it comes.

On a typical Sunday morning this vigil comes during the brief silence that takes place after the reading of the Gospel, and before the opening sentence of the sermon.

What is that vigil like? What is it like for the preacher? What is like for the members of the congregation?

For the preacher it is a combination of excitement and anxiety. Some days we are excited to preach. On others, we dread it, and can't wait for the recitation of the creed to come. That's the preacher's version of the vigil.

The congregation's vigil is a mixture also. It is a mixture of worry and hope. "Will this sermon be just more of the same old thing that I have heard countless times? Or will this sermon be a fresh word of the Lord for me today? Will it speak to my condition? Will it equip me for my journey?"

The two-sided homiletical vigil is there every time we preach. Someone once wrote that this moment between Gospel and sermon contains the greatest amount of hope and anticipation in the entire liturgy. Vigils are important. Sermons are important. Preaching is important.

All of us need guidance and help in our preaching. Sometimes our help comes from the Scriptures. In tonight's first lesson, Moses is a good model for preparing to preach. Here is a list of the things he does: Moses first goes to God. Then he gets the Word. Then Moses comes down from the mountain and faithfully delivers the Word to the people. He is so persuasive that he wins total acceptance. They say, "Everything that the Lord has spoken we will do." Moses then reports to God on what he has done and tells God about the response of the people. This leads to a dramatic manifestation of God's presence.

The Pentateuch writers combine to give us a multimedia theophany. There is fire and smoke to see and a thunderous voice to hear. In more than one way the sermon has worked. The people have listened and heard. They have been persuaded. They have sensed God's presence. Now they are prepared to shape their lives in accordance with God's will. They agree to everything that has been said, and in chapter twenty, the Ten Commandments will be given. This is one great guide for preachers. How might it work for us?

Go to God first. Pray, read, mark, learn, and inwardly digest the Scriptures. Do that until you get the Word. Find out what the Scriptures and God are saying to you. You need to be the first person to hear the sermon you are constructing for others. If you haven't received the Word yourself, the sermon may not be ready to give to anyone else.

Deliver the sermon faithfully. This means not to fudge on what you have discovered in your prayer and study. If you have been given something to say, say it! Proclaiming faithfully also means to deliver your word persuasively. We should not be ashamed to attempt to win the people over to what we believe to be a truth of God.

Last, be mindful of results. There is purpose in our preaching, just as there was purpose for Moses. We are preaching so that people will come into the nearer presence of God. We are preaching so that people will reflect on their experience with God, amend their lives on the basis of that experience, and live in such a way that they will make a difference for good in the world.

In our other lesson for this evening, the author of First Peter remembers the Sinai covenant, and uses some of the same words to give assurance and comfort to his congregation. They are experiencing stress and suffering in their lives because they are no longer able to relate comfortably to their pagan neighbors and communities. The author helps them to glory in their special status through words that we often use as descriptive of the church. "But you are a chosen race, a royal priesthood, a holy nation, God's own people. . . . Once you were not a people, but now you are God's people. Once you had not received mercy, but now you have received mercy."[1]

I sense that we really enjoy the part of this passage that is descriptive. We glory in the words "chosen race, royal priesthood, holy nation, God's own people" even as we take them to ourselves.

Less often do we emphasize the prescriptive part of the passage, in the middle of which we find words that tell us why God has made us chosen, royal, and holy. Here they are. We have been made chosen, royal, and holy "in order that you may proclaim the mighty acts of him who called you out of darkness into his marvelous light."[2]

The author of First Peter does not mince words or minimize the importance of this work. Later in the letter he writes the following about those that would stand and speak before the congregation: "Whoever speaks must do so as one speaking the very words of God."[3]

We should be committed to preaching, and preaching well. The Scriptures demand it; our people are hungry for it; and the church languishes in those places where the preaching ministry is neglected or exercised poorly.

This conference has been put together because we are committed to your preaching. Starting tonight we need to build a worshiping and preaching community. In that community, each of us should strive to be both preachers and hearers. It is not just the preached Word that heals and saves. It is the preached Word *heard*. That addition is so important. Part of what will keep you alive as a preacher will be the faithful hearers who loan you their ears and hearts. They can help you with constructive feedback so you can grow; and they will give you confirmation and strength by letting you know when and how you are getting through to them for God.

We are here to preach and to practice. Each and every sermon is an event in itself, and also an occasion for learning and growth. We need to think about our preaching and to reflect on our preaching. We will be doing a lot of that this week. We do it because experience, by itself, teaches us little. Real learning and growth only take place when experience is reflected upon and understood. This *can* be done alone. We believe it is *better* done with others in community. There are also some things that can be done after seminary is over and you are in the parish. One of them is to gather preaching colleagues and work on your preaching together. Another is to track your own preaching over the years. You will be amazed to see how it changes over time.

Many of us now have computers, and this makes it easy for us to save sermons. I would like to suggest that you keep your sermons as the years pass. After three, six, or nine years, bring up on screen the sermon you preached on a set of lessons years ago. This can be a frightening and enlightening experience. I have done this and wondered how in the world I could have stood before a congregation and said what I said way back then. I don't suggest we do this to beat ourselves up, but rather to trace and see how much we grow and change. There are lots of other things to say, but that is what this conference is for. We are so glad you are here and we hope it will be a rewarding week for you.

The time for this vigil is over. Tomorrow is the feast of the Spirit. Pray then that the Spirit will be with us this week, guide us to a sense of God's nearer presence, and help us to grow into passionate preachers of the Word of God.

Roger Alling is coeditor of this volume.

---

1. I Peter 2:9–10.

2. Ibid., v. 9b.

3. Ibid., v. 4:11a.

THE MARTYRS OF LYONS

Digging into Yourself—Finding Out about God

Mark 8:34–38
Matthew R. Lincoln

FOR THOSE OF YOU who have not yet memorized every page of *Lesser Feasts and Fasts*, let me remind you of a few details in the story of Blandina and her companions, the martyrs of Lyons. In the year 177, Christians were being persecuted in Lyons. A standard strategy of the persecutors was to capture slaves from Christian households and torture them in order to extract false accusations of scandalous, immoral behavior by their householders. This would stir up the public against otherwise respectable Roman citizens, and enable the government to persecute them, too. Blandina was such a slave. She defended herself and her household by saying simply, "I am a Christian. Nothing vile is done among us."

Perhaps it would be hard for you to make the same claim that nothing vile is done in your Christian community back home. It would be hard for me to do so about mine. Still, we preachers have something important in common with Blandina. As preachers, we are called to be *martyrs*, that is, *witnesses*. I do not mean to aggrandize our role with the hyperbolic use of an impressive word. I believe we are called to stake our lives on what we say every time we preach.

Now, what does that mean—if it does not mean risking physical attack from our hearers by what we say? It means we expose our true identity in the pulpit the way Blandina did. It took her only four words: "I am a Christian." It might take us more, but as we preach the Word we have received, the person we are necessarily comes out with the Word we preach.

I find that prospect frightening. When I was in seminary, I learned a term that described much of what I dreaded about the discernment process for ordination: "forced self-disclosure." Before I ever got to seminary, there were two different discernment committees with whom I had to share from the depths of my being. Then, more of that during seminary, and one more round for clergy new to the diocese after seminary. I found it intrusive and phony. It may have exposed me, but it did not build up either me or the church.

During that same time, however, I had a positive experience of self-disclosure in preaching that was neither intrusive nor phony. A few months after participating in the Preaching Excellence Program as a student, I began my senior year at the General Seminary and, in the usual course of events, was invited to preach in the Chapel of the Good Shepherd. I was thrilled. It was to be on my patronal feast day, St. Matthew the Apostle. But as the day drew closer, I became more and more uncomfortable trying to prepare a sermon. At the time, I was very angry with several classmates, and I found it harder and harder to think about preaching to them. The Gospel passage for the Feast of St. Matthew is about Jesus accepting the unacceptable, and I could not see how to preach that kind of acceptance to people with whom I was so angry.

A monk was visiting the campus from the Order of the Holy Cross. I grabbed him away from a cup of coffee to help me talk through my problem. I ended up repenting of the grudge I was harboring and made my first private confession to a priest. What a tremendous relief it was to be rid of that burden, and what a release of energy it was for working on my sermon! Much more, I discovered part of my identity as one forgiven and graced to forgive others.

Well, whose identity is that, really! Perhaps you remember, from your rummaging around in the gospels, all the times scribes and Pharisees were outraged when Jesus forgave someone his or her sins. The religious leaders of the day were outraged, because having the authority to forgive sins was not part of any human being's identity; except, of course, that Jesus was also the Son of God.

So, "forgiven and graced to forgive." Whose identity was that? Mine? No, I discovered not my own identity, but the identity of Christ alive in me. That is the identity we are called to disclose from the pulpit. Self-disclosure? Yes. All about me? No. All about the Christ alive in me.

Let's think a little further about how Christ is identified. In simple terms, he is most clearly identified by the cross, the means of his torture and death. Jesus is some dead guy on a cross outside a minor city a long time ago. Dead and insignificant. We can never forget that this Christ alive in us, whose identity we share, is identified by his death on the cross. So, when we hear the call to take up our cross, we are not being called to take on some burden of responsibility. We already have burdens enough. We are not being called to endure the hardships of life politely, with a smile. We are called to take up our deaths. When we take up our cross, we take up our death. I had to take up my death to preach that sermon. I had to let my anger die, even though it might have been well founded. That is how I discovered, in a way that I believed—in a way that shaped the world differently for me at that moment—the gospel Word I was being given to preach.

Carrying your cross, which is both identifying with Christ and carrying your death, is witnessing, staking your life on what you stand for when you preach, being a martyr. My understanding of who I am, my identity, was all over that sermon. But notice what being a martyr in the pulpit is *not*: it is not forced self-disclosure. It is not intrusive, or giving up privacy. Notice what I have not told you: I have not told you why I was mad at my friends. I have not told you what I said in my confession or what the priest said to me. I have not told you how it went with those friends after that. I have not hung my laundry all over the pulpit. Those things are private and are not necessary for you to see my witness, the presence of my identity in Christ, in the sermon.

Here's what being a martyr in the pulpit is. It is delving into yourself and confronting the issues in your life that are confronted by the gospel; and when you have done that, showing your people not what you found out about yourself, but what you found out about God. To be a martyr in your preaching is to show that God has raised you from the dead, that God loved you as you were before you died, loved you in your death, and loves you now in your new life in Christ. In delving into your life, you offer it to God as a martyr does, confident that God will receive this dying life and, through your preaching, give it to the church, risen and alive in Christ.

Matthew R. Lincoln is Rector of St. John's Church,
North Haven, Connecticut.

EVENSONG

Cartoons and the Kingdom

Matthew 13:44–52
Joy E. Rogers

"Have you understood all this?"

That's how Jesus ends a sermon.

After nearly a chapter full of parables, undoubtedly powerfully preached, he says,

"Have you understood all this?" They answered, "Yes."

Oh, come on! Wouldn't you bet they were lying? Or at least, merely being polite. "Lovely message, Rabbi, so inspiring."

Far be it from me to call into question Jesus' effectiveness as a preacher. But don't you ever wonder if Peter and James and Mary Magdalene and the rest of that crew might have done better with something a bit more concrete?

Parables feel a little elusive for your average disciple. It seems to me that much of what transpires in the next dozen or so chapters of Matthew's Gospel indicates that this oh-so-understanding crew of disciples were still pretty "unclear on the concept," however great the preacher.

My preaching career had a humble beginning. I was a senior seminarian working Sundays in a parish. I helped them start a children's liturgy. You know the drill—prayers, homily, lessons, all more accessible to the three-to-seven-year-old set than what was happening in "big church." The kids joined the others at the Peace, for Eucharist. Things went swimmingly for nearly six months. Then the rector noticed that I rarely showed up in the adult service until the Peace. "You need to do your part in the parish liturgy for the sake of your own formation," he said.

I didn't know how to tell him that, as a lowly seminarian, I was scheduled to preach in his arena only every two or even three months. I was a bigger fish in the little pond; the children's liturgy team was more than willing to let me "preach" virtually every week. I confessed my obsession. The rector was amused. "Fine," he said. "But telling cute stories to the kids is scarcely the same as preaching."

He was right. I didn't add that telling cute stories to grownups might not be preaching either. I only knew that I was hooked. I had glimpsed the pearl of great price—this preaching thing. Any reasonably attentive crew of Christians would do for me. The next issue was what I could do for them.

A veteran preacher wrote: "It is of great importance for Christian believers to have, from time to time, a reasonable, sane, mature person stand up in their midst and say, 'God is . . .,' and go on to complete the sentence intelligibly."[1]

Was it less important just because these Christian believers were under the age of seven? I thought I was reasonable, sane, and mature. And at least smart enough to recognize that this young congregation was teaching basic homiletics to a rookie preacher.

There is more give and take with the Romper Room set than you find in your average collection of proper Episcopalians. This crew didn't vote with their feet if they were bored. They voted with their whole bodies. That is why we had one adult assigned to accompany any child with a bored bladder to the restroom. And another to deal with bored elbows that were nudging neighbors. Not every congregation offers such amenities.

There is no such thing as a rhetorical question with five-year-olds. My first disaster came early on. The creation story. "How were Adam and Eve made?" I asked in honeyed tones. We listened with fascination as a precocious child told us how tiny sperm swim and swim to find the lonely egg. An important lesson—good biology is not always adequate theology.

There was not much temptation to preach your exegesis. This bunch loved Noah's ark. J, E, D, and P belonged on alphabet blocks. They were *real* sure about Jesus, surer than I was some days. After all they had known him since he was a baby. They liked the kind of person he became when he grew up.

They were less sure about how it is with God. They couldn't say omnipotence or theodicy. They knew about hurt, and loss, and fear, and grief. They wondered about a God who let the world work so badly sometimes.

The prayers of these little people were graphic.

Please help my daddy stop drinking.
Please make my mommy stop crying.
Don't let my gramma die,—or my dog, or my goldfish, or my hamster.
My friend has AIDS; I'm not allowed to play with him; please make him better.

Cute stories couldn't cut it. How do you say "God is" to kids—in a way that God isn't reduced to a pet or rendered insipid or turned into a cosmic bogeyman? How do you say "God is" to anyone? We all need someone to keep us thinking about God, rather than just making random guesses. And to leave us with hope that we live in a creation, not a madhouse.[1]

The Kingdom of heaven is like . . .

"Jesus teaches by parables," I told my young congregation. "Do you understand all this?"

"Yes," they said. I knew they weren't being merely polite.

A six-year-old theologian continued my sermon. "Jesus talks in cartoons," he announced. The rest solemnly nodded. They couldn't say hermeneutics either, but they had an interpretive lens for these Jesus tales. It wasn't about "getting the point"; it was about living in another kind of world for a little while.

My cartoon consciousness had been formed by what you might call the classics of the genre. We found intergenerational connections in the likes of Mickey Mouse and Donald Duck, Bugs Bunny and Elmer Fudd, Tweety Bird and Sylvester. The ever-popular Roadrunner and his would-be nemesis, Wile E. Coyote. All that was asked of anyone who would enter the topsy-turvy realm of the cartoonist was a willing suspension of disbelief. Not a bad standard for any would-be worshiper.

Children knew how to move into these worlds of singing mice and dancing ducks, creatures who have girlfriends and nephews and jobs and houses, just like us. They saw that Mickey and Donald are as likely to fall prey to their own ignorance, carelessness, or ambitions as they are to be threatened by fantastic enemies—just like us.

Cartoon characters defy gravity, mortality, and biology. Not at all like us. All manner of beasties are human in their personas, superhuman in their possibilities. They run off cliffs and do not fall, until they remember that they are no longer on solid ground. They crash to the canyon floor, are smashed flat by the bulldozer, or blown up by dynamite. The smashed and the crashed and the blown-to-smithereens are vividly, even engagingly, portrayed in their defeat and then immediately repaired for more of the same.

The cartoon cosmos is filled with action-packed struggle. Good always prevails. But good is not wholly innocent. The sweet canary and the rascally rabbit are pretty canny—ingenious, shrewd, and resourceful. (Wise as serpents and innocent as doves?)

And they are the habitual quarries of some likable and repeatedly hapless villains. Elmer Fudd puts in long hours tramping through the forest, shouldering his trusty shotgun, inspired by visions of a lunch of barbecued bunny. Sylvester the alley cat salivates at the mere sight and sound of the delectable little bird and risks life and limb in pursuit of a gourmet hors d'oeuvre.

Those hungers that would harm another are perpetually unsatisfied is an integral rule of this realm. Evil is always defeated in cartoonland but never destroyed. Violence is prevalent but never, never ultimate.

These kids helped me see how they enter a cartoon world and find it alive with lasting tensions and constant struggle, a realm of danger and delight, but one that is ultimately safe for all its inhabitants—where each experience is brought to a happy consummation without ever denying the possibility that there may be more to come.

A cartoon Kingdom defies the physical universe, because its Creator says so. New and inexplicable rules apply to residents of the realm. The artists do not ask us to extrapolate natural principles to guide our own lives, but to enjoy the prospects of another order and allow ourselves to live there for a moment. You do not need to run off a cliff, dance with a duck, and seek the lair of a "wascally wabbit" to open your imagination to the creative possibilities of a world that works another way. And maybe something is changed in that. Maybe you are.

The Kingdom of heaven is like . . ., says Jesus to his friends.

My kids knew that Jesus animates a realm where little things count, like mustard seeds and a widow's mite and children and incarnations. Where the least of creatures, like prostitutes and tax collectors and Samaritans, and even you and me, cannot escape the fine mesh of the great net that will bring us all home. Jesus shows us the place where what is lost will always be found, like prodigal sons and straying sheep and hidden treasures and lives lost for the sake of others. Where seekers and searchers of all kinds will be given more than they sought, like kings and peasants alike who sought a Jewish king and found instead the Lord of glory, like women looking for the dead body of their friend who find instead a risen Savior. The parable Kingdom defies a social universe, because the Creator does so, overturning the rules of custom, culture, and common sense.

The Kingdom of heaven is like . . .

Jesus doesn't ask us to extrapolate moral principles or plan new programs with these tales. He wants us to enjoy the presence of God and discover the purposes of God, in our own adventures in gospel land. His parables are challenges to open our hearts and imaginations to the prospects of another order, and invitations to live there with him here and now.

The youngest members of the Body were perhaps the most skilled at living in the world that Jesus animates for us all. Violence is still real and prevalent there, but even the utter violence of a cross is never, never ultimate. Evil is defeated, but nothing of God's creation is destroyed. An empty tomb marks a happy consummation without ever denying the possibility that there is more, much more, to come.

The Kingdom of heaven is like . . .

A group of kids taught a beginner a long time ago that becoming a preacher is not about "getting it," but about living there. It is about moving into another realm for the moment, or for eternity, and letting it work its mystery and magic on soul and psyche; and then daring to report on what you have seen there and whom you have met. To put to the test our perceptions of ourselves as reasonable, sane, and mature, making gospel norms, not the culture's, the measure of our reason and our sanity and our wisdom. To risk saying "God is" to Christian believers, because we have found the treasure, glimpsed the pearl of great price, been caught up ourselves in a net of grace and gift with the rest of a fishy company.

Like a cartoon coyote, we all will chase an elusive sermon right over the edge of the cliff and discover in the middle of the abyss that there is no solid ground beneath us as we plunge helplessly to earth. Like Elmer Fudd, we will still plod along, salivating at the prospect of homiletical perfection, no matter how often our aims are defeated by our own egos or our own considerable capacities to be unclear on the concept. And like the "wascally wabbit," we can live unafraid, offer our best, delight in the challenges, and revel in the sheer adventure of it all. Because we are residents of a realm where violence is never ultimate, where goodness and God will one day prevail, where a preacher regularly finds riches beyond her wildest dreams, and where there is always more, much more to come.

Have you understood all this?

Joy E. Rogers is Rector of St. Thomas Church, Battle Creek, Michigan.

---

1. Eugene H. Peterson, *Reversed Thunder: The Revelation of John and the Praying Imagination* (San Francisco: HarperCollins, 1988), 4.

VISITATION OF THE VIRGIN MARY

Preaching from the Soles of Your Feet

Colossians 3:12–17; Luke 1:39–49
Charles Rice

THIS STORY of Mary's visit to Elizabeth, like the movable feast that we call the Excellence in Preaching Conference, presents us with a wonderful convergence. Filled with the Spirit of Pentecost, with homilies (and hush puppies!) replete, finding our place in this way-out hill country, with plenty of porches and time for visiting, we should be able to enter into Luke's narrative. One could hardly imagine a more fitting text for those trying to entertain and serve the Word of God.

At the same time that Mary receives the news, the divine messenger tells her that her kinswoman Elizabeth, in her old age, is six months pregnant. When Mary is ten weeks along, or so, she goes to the backcountry village where Elizabeth is confined, being within a month or so of John's birth.

How to picture this? Many of us would see a nice house in the country, an older woman looking pleased, sitting in her rocker, hands folded on a very large belly, no doubt a little frazzled, both eager and anxious. The younger woman, hardly showing, greets Elizabeth, and whatever it is that she says causes the unborn John to leap in the womb at the mere proximity of the one to whom his whole life will be tied. In two pregnant women and a child kicking in his mother's womb we see—do we not?—an unmistakable picture of what it is to be a preacher of the Gospel.

As every seminarian knows, the great preacher of Boston, Philips Brooks, gave preaching a definition that has stuck: "Preaching is the communication of Truth through personality." Just so we would not misunderstand, Brooks capitalized the word *Truth*. If Brooks had a computer he would put it in bold face: **Preaching is God's Truth coming to us through real human beings.**

Today, we might want to change "personality" to "personhood," given the undue preoccupation of American culture with personalities. Be that as it may, Brooks has given us a lasting definition of preaching: the eternal Word of God, manifest in the One born of Mary, comes into the world again, constantly, amazingly, through you. Your unique and unrepeatable biography. Your inimitable voice. Your peculiar sins and failures. And your particular use of the means of grace.

In Brooks' definition, it is just where, in our oh-so-human lives—where we are placed with the people and occasions given to us—that we receive the Word so it gets spoken in a way that can be heard. John—unborn, in the womb, weak and vulnerable like his large, old mother—is the vehicle of the saving Word coming into the world, through Mary, and John, and the likes of you and me.

One of the great preachers of this century and a teacher of mine, Edmund Steimle, put it to our class one day. It must have been one of those days when—as sometimes happens in practice preaching classes or on a summer morning in church—we were going through the motions, giving homilies as if they were no more than academic assignments. "Charles, you have to preach from the soles of your feet."

He insisted, in his classes at Union Theological Seminary, on a full text in the pulpit, and the most thoroughgoing preparation of each sermon; but with that he listened for an authentic voice true to this person in this moment. A tall order.

It is John, hearing the voice of the one who will bear Jesus into the world, bounding in Elizabeth's womb. It is Elizabeth, filled with the Spirit and overcome with amazement and gratitude at what has come into her house. It is Mary: "My soul magnifies the Lord, and my Spirit rejoices. . . ."

From the soles of their feet.

With my whole being. In spite of, and because of, and with the help of everything that has ever happened to me, I preach the Word which takes on human flesh and dwells among us. And calls us, each of us, in the words of today's Epistle, to "let the Word of Christ dwell in us richly."[1]

With these pregnant women and this unborn prophet, in our own humanity, here and now, we receive the redeeming Christ with our whole being. And right there, from the soles of our feet, preach this saving Word.

Joseph Sittler spoke of this as "the anguish of preaching," in a book by that title:

Preaching is not merely something a preacher does; it is a function of the preacher's whole existence concentrated at the point of declaration and interpretation.[2]

I remember vividly the first time I heard Edmund Steimle preach in chapel at Union. Vested in cassock and surplice, he came down the aisle at the procession, wearing penny loafers as he always did in class and around the campus. Preaching: the communication of the Truth, from the soles of our feet, in penny loafers. That's it, according to Philips Brooks and Edmund Steimle, and Mary and Elizabeth and John.

I've been thinking about Oxford, Mississippi, the last few days. Just coming to this state evokes William Faulkner and his enduring characters. In his novel, *The Sound and the Fury*, we see yet another woman, heavy on her feet, heaving herself up and down the steps of the big southern house at the whim of the effete and declining Compsons. But in the overheated kitchen, subject to a chaotic and abusive family, Dilsey not only endures, but rejoices in the perfect freedom of those who serve Christ. On Sunday she takes the feebleminded child, Benjy, and goes off to the ramshackle clapboard church with its peeling paint and aged preacher. Over the pulpit is a faded paper Christmas bell, the kind that folds up like an accordion. Here, with the signs all around her of the world that is passing away, Dilsey speaks quietly to herself the Word that gets her through: "I've seen the first and the last, the beginning and the end, the Alpha and the Omega."

There, in the back country of Mississippi, a black woman hears and receives the Word of God, and in her own hard place bears her faithful witness to the One without whom nothing came to be and toward whose purposes all things, however imperceptibly, are moving.

Bishop Duncan Gray also told us on Tuesday evening about Oxford, where he was rector of St. Peter's Church, in the early 1960s. When James Meredith knocked at the door of Old Miss, the young priest took his side and told his parishioners that they should do the same. The result was abandonment of priest and parish by many, and hate mail and threats from across the state.

In answer to the question—"How did you do that? Your life was in danger, and probably the lives of your family. Where did you get the courage to do what you did?"—his answer was unforgettable: "It was really quite simple. I was an Episcopal priest in Oxford, Mississippi, in 1962."

That is it, is it not, for those of us who would be pastors and preachers and even prophets? The call is to receive the gift as faithfully and gratefully as do Mary and Elizabeth, in their particular times and places, and to respond with all we have, like a child leaping in the womb. Or a young priest standing up and speaking out on a Sunday morning in Oxford, Mississippi, in 1962.

This, of course, is not only the calling of those who put on stoles and stand at the altar, though we do have a special role among Christ's people in the service of God's Word. The Word dwells richly in God's people, whose life we are privileged to embody and to carry with love and gratitude to altar and pulpit and place of prayer.

But this saving Word draws near to Dilsey and to Duncan, to men and women, girls and boys everywhere who try to listen and to speak, to take into ourselves and to body forth in the world the saving Word.

The Delta agent, a calm African-American man, could see how tired I was, still trying to get a flight to Jackson at five in the morning. As he rewrote my ticket, he asked what was taking me to Mississippi; and I told him about you and this conference.

Then he handed me the new ticket and wished me a good time "with all those preachers." Walking to the gate, I glanced at the envelope. He had written, next to the number of the gate: "Be encouraged, brother. Ephesians 3:20."

Listen to it, preachers. It is what we see in Mary and Elizabeth and John. In Dilsey and Duncan, and a Delta agent. And it is what we need to hear every time we try, once more, to receive and to bear the Word of God.

Now to him who by the power at work within us is able to do far more abundantly than all that we ask or think, to him be glory in the church and in Christ Jesus to all generations, forever and ever. Amen

Charles Rice is Professor of Homiletics in the Divinity School of Drew University, Madison, New Jersey.

---

1. Colossians 3:16.
2. John Sittler, *The Anguish of Preaching* (Minneapolis: Fortress, 1966), 8.

Evensong

God Vision

Ecclesiastes 2:16–26; Matthew 13:53–58
Lucy Lind Hogan

The rush of the Divine Breath is always echoing in our ears. "Receive the Holy Spirit." The Holy Spirit has come upon us, filling us, strengthening us, empowering us—awakening us to God's presence and power. God is here, with us, in us. Do we see? Do we hear? Do we understand and trust that *God is*?

This evening, as the shadows lengthen and the busy world is hushed, we have an opportunity to reflect upon God's presence and upon our problems with perceiving that presence. Perception of sensory data is an interesting thing. It is clear that, as one grows older, our eyes weaken and our hearing dims. However, no matter what our age, old or young, we do not always see clearly or hear correctly. So many things get in our way.

Before I painted with words, I painted with colors; and I taught others to draw and paint. I taught my students how to "squint." What is the squint? Have you ever painted a picture or a wall? Have you ever hung a picture? Then perhaps you have squinted. You squinted and moved your head from side to side, backing up, moving forward, to change your perspective. To get a different view, to change your perception.

Try that now. Pick a spot on the wall, a person. Look at them with your head straight, your eyes wide open. Now, squint your eyes and move your head as you return and look at that same spot.

What happened? Did you see it differently?

When we look, do we really see? When we listen do we really hear?

How often we have problems with our perception. Our minds and hearts trick us into seeing things that are not there. Or ignoring things that are. We correct, or ignore, faults. This reality is important as we hear the words of Qoheleth and Matthew.

"Vanity, Vanity, all is Vanity." Who am I? What is my place in this world? What endures? Fame? Fortune? Wisdom? Talent? Beauty? Genius? What must we do to ensure that we will have a lasting impact on our world? What must we do to ensure that no one will forget us, that we will be remembered long after we are gone? How can we make sure that our legacy will be respected, valued, admired, and esteemed?

We cringe when we hear the words of Qoheleth, "There is no enduring remembrance of the wise or of fools, seeing that in the days to come all will have been long forgotten."[1]

The truth is clear. God is our alpha and our omega, our beginning and our end. The things of this world will pass away, and we, like the grass of the field, will pass away, but "the Word of our God will stand for ever."[2] "This God is our God for ever and ever; this God shall be our guide for evermore."[3]

But we have problems with our perception, and we begin to think that *we* are the beginning and the end.

Much of our fascination with the wreck of the *Titanic,* I believe, lies in its ability to confront us with the fragility, the transitory nature of our human existence. Wealth, power, fame could not prevent those people from death. As we sit in the darkened theater watching that enormous vessel, that pinnacle of human engineering, slide into the icy water, the words of Qoheleth confront us with the uncomfortable reality of our lives. We work, we struggle, we build; in the end it is for nought.

> *How can the wise die just like fools? . . . I hated all my toil in which I had toiled under the sun, seeing that I must leave it to those who come after me—and who knows whether they will be wise or foolish? Yet they will be master of all for which I toiled and used my wisdom under the sun.*
> *Vanity of vanities! All is vanity.*[4]

We want to believe that we are in charge, we are in control. We want to believe that we are responsible for all that happens to us. We take great pleasure in pointing out, "I built that. I made that. I did that. That happened because I made it happen."

The preacher realized that human strength, human power, human victory were not enough to guarantee success now and forever. One does not have to live very long before one sees towering giants fall. Suharto of Indonesia, apartheid in South Africa, the Soviet Union. Our success is but a little while, and then we are gone, and must leave everything to those who come after us.

We can be left to the despair of the preacher in the opening of chapter two. If we put our trust solely in human power and human strength, then surely we will be discouraged and disillusioned.

But, if we change our perception, Qoheleth reminds us, we will see that our work is really God's work. God's strength, God's power, God's victory are what endures. Do we not perceive it? We must learn to perceive God's eternity, not human finiteness. What we have is from God's hand, and when we open the eyes of our heart to see God's graciousness, "God gives wisdom and knowledge and joy."[5]

Matthew tells us that shortly before the death of John the Baptizer, Jesus returned to his home and began teaching in the synagogue. What is it like to go home? Some of you are fortunate to have parents who are still alive. What happens when you go to visit your family, your relatives? Do they still treat you like children—no matter what your age? Some of us have children who come home to visit. It is hard not to continue to treat them like the children of yours that they are.

A few weeks ago my husband and I returned to the Twin Cities to visit my parents and attend our twenty-fifth college reunion. Fascinating things happen to you and to those around you when you return home.

Jesus was preaching—but his friends and neighbors had a problem with perception. The Good News of God's truth was enfleshed in their friend, their neighbor, and their old school classmate.

"Who does he think he is?" They found it difficult to hear through Jesus to God's Word. "Where did this man get this wisdom and these deeds of power? Is not this the carpenter's son? Is not his mother called Mary?" They still lived with his brothers and sisters—"Why should we listen to him?"

They saw only what they wanted to see. They could not get beyond their old perceptions of Jesus, the man with whom they had grown up. They could not see the Word incarnate. They could not see the Word made flesh. They could not hear the Good News. They could not accept his miracles of healing. They could not perceive God working in their midst.

In his letter to the Christians in Corinth, Paul reminds us that problems with perception are part of being human: "For now we see in a mirror, dimly, but then we will see face to face. Now I know only in part; then I will know fully, even as I have been fully known."[6]

Our perceptions of the world around us, of family, friends, neighbors, strangers, of God's presence, are all clouded and incomplete. We need to learn *not* to trust our first perception. Qoheleth, Matthew, and Paul urge us to look more closely, to listen more intently, to put behind us the prejudices and preconceived ideas that constrain and imprison us.

Jesus, Matthew tells us, "did not do many deeds of power" in his hometown—not because he could not, but because they *would not* see. Likewise, the risen Christ cannot do many deeds of power in our lives if we *will not* see.

Squinting, which is an invaluable tool of artists, must become an important part of our prayer life. It is our God Vision. We must learn to step back and squint at our lives. When we squint we make a critical assessment, we see what is still awry, what we have missed. In that moment we see differently, experiencing the wholeness of the moment, accepting our limitations and finitude, by blurring the boundaries between us and the rest of God's creation. Squinting forces us to see that there are other perspectives, other connections, other patterns possible.

The Good News is that we do not have to remain limited by our problems of perception. The Good News is that the grace of God, working in and through us, opens our hearts and minds to perceive God in our midst, so that with the Psalmist we may declare,

> *This God is our God for ever and ever;*
> *This God shall be our guide for evermore.*[7]

Lucy Lind Hogan is Associate Professor of Homiletics at Wesley Theological Seminary, Washington, D.C.

---

1. Ecclesiastes 2:16a.
2. Isaiah 40:8b.
3. Psalm 48:13.
4. Ecclesiastes 2:16b, 18–19; 1:2b.
5. Ecclesiastes 2:26a.
6. 1 Corinthians 13:12.
7. Psalm 48:13.

EMBER DAY

Journey into Compassion

Matthew 9:35–38
Lisa Kraske Cressman

THEY WERE a mess. They were just a mess.

They were hungry. They were ignorant. They suffered from terrible illnesses and the deaths of their loved ones. They wondered where God was. What would God do for them? It certainly didn't look like much.

Jesus saw their suffering. Their wounds, inside and out. He saw their illnesses, their ignorance. He saw their grief. But he knew where God was, and what God was doing. And it was considerable. God was suffering, crying, and grieving with them. So Jesus gave them hopeful Words of God to dam the flood of their despair. He gave them instructions on how to live in order to stem the tide of their ignorance. He touched them to stop the flow of their wounds. And he felt it all. Their despair and their hope. Their ignorance, and their freedom that results from knowledge. Their illness, and their joy in healing. He did all that he could. Jesus taught and preached and healed.

But still the suffering went on. The suffering went on, and he couldn't get to them all. The need was too great and the days too short. Yet still the suffering meant that he simply must act. He felt compelled by sympathy to do something. Do something more than he already was doing.

So Jesus turned to the disciples. He told them to notice, to see, to feel the suffering. He told the disciples to go to work. Go to work in the midst of the people to become aware, to experience, to perceive, to be so moved by compassion that they, too, would teach and preach and heal. What the disciples did not yet know was that Jesus had just started them on a lifelong journey into the heart of compassion.

That Jesus got them started on that journey at all was because God had perceived the heartbreaking consequences of creatureliness that caused illness and death. God had amassed the suffering caused by humans' poor choices. God knew and absorbed it all. Every tear, every hunger pang, every illness, every parting by death. God gathered it all. And God was so moved by it, so filled with compassion, that God desired to be among us, to live in solidarity with the suffering. In compassion God came to the physical world as an infant so that God would live with us in vulnerability and dependence.

In Jesus, God's compassion and desire to act were embodied in flesh. Jesus would know and feel the limits of gravity, of food, of time, and of mortality with us and for us. And Jesus would act. He would perceive the need, and then teach and preach and heal. He would lament and mourn and weep with us. And then, to carry on this compassionate work, Jesus would empower disciples to go and do likewise. They were to go and journey literally among the suffering. And by journeying with the suffering, they would also journey into the heart of God's compassion for them and for the world.

How can we understand what God's compassion is? What is this compassion that Jesus held so deeply? Looking at Jesus' acts of compassion throughout the Gospels, we can discern what his compassion encompassed. Jesus held an *agape*-type love for others. He pondered people's living conditions and held an active regard for their best welfare. Jesus often felt a long-lasting and intense emotional reaction. And all of that, the love, pondering, active regard, and intense feeling, consolidated into action.

Twice he fed crowds of thousands. He healed countless people. He raised others from the dead. He told parables to jolt the listeners from their complacency. He taught in synagogues and preached Good News. At times, he simply stood in solidarity when nothing else was to be done. And finally, he gathered to himself all the suffering that ever was and ever would be and died with it to ensure that suffering and death would never have ultimate power.

Another way to describe Jesus' compassion that compelled him to act is in the words of John Ruusbroec: "Compassion is a wounding of the heart which love extends to all without distinction."[1] We know ourselves and our own lives well enough to be able to name a few of the ways in which Jesus' own wounding of the heart, *because* of us, was extended in love even to us.

Every time we journey to the Eucharistic table, Jesus' compassion and subsequent actions are what we commemorate and celebrate. We digest the very heart of compassion in broken bread and mixed wine. We journey more deeply into the mystery of why God would care enough to send Jesus. We journey more deeply into the mystery of why Jesus would care about us. Of why Jesus cares about us enough to allow his heart, in the same moment, to be broken by us, even while extending that same heart to embrace us. We journey more deeply into accepting Christ's compassion. And all of that consolidates in us so that we, too, are willing to be wounded by others' suffering, and then willing to extend Jesus' compassion to all without distinction.

This wounding of the heart extended in love to all has profound implications for our ministries. We as ministers today are no less harried and helpless than the people Jesus encountered. The church is in a difficult time of massive transition. The mainline churches are no longer so mainline, if determined by sheer numbers. Some are even calling us "old-line" churches. A consumer mentality for religion, lack of denominational identity, a litigious society directed even toward the church and the church insurance company—all these have us scrambling. We don't know what it means to be church when children's soccer tournaments are scheduled against Sunday services. We need Jesus' compassion, his teaching, preaching, and healing in new and different ways than we ever have before.

And yet in other ways, we don't need anything new. To notice and feel, to see and perceive the needs, to experience the suffering so that we are compelled to act or to stand in solidarity is no different from the disciples. The world today needs compassion no less and no more than it did two thousand years ago.

People are still hungry. We are still ignorant. We still suffer from terrible illnesses. People still wonder who God is and what God can do. And Jesus, out of compassion, still sends us out to get to work. But to minister to the needs of the world with integrity means we need to allow Jesus' compassion for our own personal plights of hunger, ignorance, illness, and doubts to have enfolded and transformed us. We need to journey into the heart of Jesus' compassion even while we seek to minister in his name.

One of the most vibrant examples of one who ministered with compassion, one whose own wounding of the heart was extended in love to those he served without distinction, was a priest with whom I served in Berkeley while I was in seminary at the Church Divinity School of the Pacific.

Steve Brannon, his wife Barbara, and their mentally handicapped young-adult daughter, Heather, served and lived in the Episcopal Campus Ministry of Canterbury House in Berkeley, California, for seven years. The three of them lived in some of the most cramped quarters that I've ever seen: two tiny bedrooms and a microscopic bathroom. Their twenty-five years of marriage had accumulated the usual paraphernalia, most of which was required to remain in boxes stacked floor to ceiling, consuming nearly every available inch of wall space. It was all the space they had to themselves. They shared the living room and kitchen with twenty-five or so students. Not easy for a couple of Myers-Briggs introverts.

It wasn't that Steve couldn't find another job. He sought out this call. He had seen that the Cal-Berkeley students weren't receiving adequate ministerial attention. They were harassed and in many ways helpless, as wounded young adults. Steve believed that to live in solidarity with their poverty, in solidarity with their uncomfortable, run-down living conditions was what was needed. It was out of compassion that he sought the position.

There were a number of costs to his compassion. He could have made more money in a parish position. In addition, there was a significant dip in his pension because the diocese paid close to the minimum for their campus ministers, in spite of Steve's many years of ordained experience. He also could have made more money by using his additional credentialing as a lawyer in a fashion more lucrative than serving immigrants and the indigent. There was, moreover, the subtle cost of receiving little respect, as a campus minister, from parochial clergy. He had no visibility to be tapped for diocesan positions.

Steve perceived the needs of students. He knew through a life of deep and consistent prayer that God loved and forgave him. And so he was moved by compassion to live with and serve the students. He was often compelled to small acts of compassion, like teaching a young man how to set a table properly before a home-cooked dinner date, and then consoling that student hours later after the student had *burned* said dinner! And very often he was the steady presence of solidarity while many students came to grips with their earlier lives of childhood sexual abuse. It was compassion that drove him to campus ministry, where his deep joy as a child of God met the growing pains of many young, searching adults.

Steve journeyed into compassion in his relationship with God and with the students. It can be so for all of us as human beings and ministers as well. Rather than be led by ambition, or ego, or others' expectations, we can instead, journey into compassion. To do so means that we place ourselves before God in vulnerability. We let ourselves be engulfed by God's bruised and loving heart. We let ourselves be wounded by the messy suffering of the world. And then we allow ourselves to be called to serve anyone without distinction, to whom God would send us.

Embraced by Jesus' compassion for us. Called to extend that same compassion to all others. Therein lies our lifelong journey into the heart of God's compassion.

Lisa Kraske Cressman is Associate Rector of
Trinity Church, Indianapolis, Indiana.

---

1. *Weavings*, vol. V, no. 6 (November/December 1990), 24. Quoted from *The Spiritual Espousals and Other Works*, trans. and intro. by James A. Wiseman, OSB (Mahwah, New Jersey: Paulist Press, 1985), 60.

EVENSONG

The Courage to Preach

Ecclesiastes 3:1–15; Galatians 2:11–21
Joe G. Burnett

SCENE: Somewhere in our preaching life, Sunday morning after church, greeting parishioners at the door.

An accountant: "Hey, good to see you today . . ."

A realtor, who comes once a month: "Good sermon, padre . . ."

A withered little lady who is often seen wandering the streets at odd hours: "Father, I—how are you?—I left a little plastic container of fruit salad in the refrigerator in the kitchen; it has your name on it. . . . Now don't forget it. . . ."

Oh, now here comes one—the retired professor at a moderate Southern Baptist seminary, who recently converted to the Episcopal Church and loves it. You'd kill for a compliment from him. He says: "Hey, how are you? How's your husband? Great day, isn't it?"

A verger: "Do you know that when you stand in the pulpit the banner standard looks like it's sticking out of your left ear?"

The senior warden: "You picked the hymns today! They were some of my favorites. By the way, we need to touch base before vestry this week; will you be in tomorrow?"

The somewhat off-the-wall son of a wealthy parishioner, who makes his way to the Eucharist about once or twice a year with his aging mother: "I have taken the liberty to write you a note about your sermon." He hands you the note and walks away. You read the note: "I don't understand how you can preach an Easter season sermon and not mention the name of Jesus Christ any more than you did. Am I missing something?"

What are we to do with these people? Well, we have two choices.

We can ignore them. It's the well-worn advice of a lot of seasoned preachers I have talked to. "Don't pay any attention," they say. "Passing remarks at the door are worthless. I get my feedback in other ways."

Our other choice is to listen to them—listen carefully. Sooner or later, we just may hear something that will renew in us the courage to preach.

A college-age choir member you thought only chewed gum and studied his music for the offertory anthem will come out some morning and ask you for a tape of that sermon you preached on doubting Thomas.

A recently widowed man you have ministered to will grip your hand on All Saints Sunday and tell you he's beginning to get over his grief and pick up the pieces of his life. Come by for a cup of coffee, he'll say.

A divorced woman with two small children, a former Roman Catholic—studying for a doctorate in psychology—will appear one day in your congregation and announce in jubilant tones as she greets you at the door that she has just received communion for the first time in twenty years. It was your sermon. It was like an engraved invitation to her to come to the Table. And you will smile and be suitably humbled, and then when she is gone you will mutter under your breath, "What did I say? I hardly had time to scribble a few notes. What did I say?"

Listening to these people can renew in us the courage to preach. That's a deliberate play on the title of a recent book by Parker Palmer called *The Courage to Teach.*[1] Preachers stand to learn a lot from his insight. Substitute *preach* for *teach* in a few of Palmer's theses and see what I mean:

- We preach who we are.
- Technique is what preachers use until the real preacher arrives, and this book is about helping that person show up.
- Good preaching cannot be reduced to technique; good preaching comes from the identity and integrity of the preacher.

What does it mean to have the courage to preach?

Have you ever heard the old saying that there are two kinds of people in the world—those who divide the world into two kinds of people, and those who don't? At the risk of oversimplification, I'm going to do a lot of dividing into two kinds, in the hope of expanding your imagination about the nature of the preaching task.

I believe the courage to preach rests in an understanding of how people function in two different worlds. How they are confronted with two different gospels. And how we as proclaimers of the Word must embrace the *source* of our identity and integrity; and, in so doing, choose between two different kinds of preaching.

First, who are these people, and what is their world like?

I can't help but think of my own congregation. Their world looks a lot like the one portrayed by the writer of Ecclesiastes, the speaker of the assembly, Qoheleth. I believe you've had the pleasure.

It all sounds so hopeful at first, like that song from the sixties that immortalized this text: "To everything, turn, turn, turn, there is a season, turn, turn, turn, and a time for every purpose under heaven." When I heard that song, I felt the world was mine, baby, mine! There was time for every one of my purposes under heaven!

From Sheol, Qoheleth must have laughed: "Hah, vanity!" The Hebrew word used is *hebel*: it means vapor, something insubstantial, something futile.

For to regard the world at face value may seem romantic at first, but ultimately it is idolatrous. The flip side of this is to demonize the world and try to escape it. People in our congregations, like the nervous rabbis who tried in vain to keep old Qoheleth out of the Hebrew canon, are often deep into this maneuver. Ironically, they use religion as their main escape mechanism. And again old Qoheleth shouts, "*Hebel!*"

The other world view that springs from the observations of the speaker is one of profound humility. We find ourselves in the presence of divine mystery, without pretension or presumption. Given the choice of manipulating the world, or striving to possess it or seeking to deny it, we simply stand in it in utter dependence. We yield all, we confess all, we surrender all. As Robert Farrar Capon has reminded us this morning, we die.

Two views of the world: *My* world—turn, turn, turn. Or *God's* world, in which we can take nothing for granted, especially God.

Now, two different kinds of gospels for people who see themselves living in two different worlds.

One gospel primarily promises two things: *protection* and *preservation*. If we can't figure out what in the world God is doing in the world, then give us incantations, codes of conduct, and ritual acts that will steel us for the cycles of life and maybe even curry God's favor. And to be sure we can identify who's for us and who's against us, give us some bottom line, in-or-out, up-or-down membership requirements.

Paul wants none of this. He's been there and done that. In Galatians he is astonished that some have turned to what he calls "a different gospel—*not that there is another gospel*," he adds. Then he says, "Even if we or an angel from heaven should proclaim to you a gospel contrary to what we proclaimed to you, let that one be accursed!"[2]

He puts it this way: "It is no longer I who live, but it is Christ who lives in me. And the life I now live in the flesh I live by faith in the Son of God, who loved me and gave himself for me."[3]

This is the gospel that people need—the gospel of freedom, the gospel of hope, the gospel of love. This is the gospel of God's secret activity "from the beginning to the end," which Qoheleth had said we could not find out: "It is no longer I who live, but it is Christ who lives in me."

Last Sunday in parishes and missions around this church, and tonight, we prayed this collect:

> *O God, you opened the way of eternal life to every race and nation by the promised gift of your Holy Spirit: Shed abroad this gift throughout the world by the preaching of the Gospel, that it may reach to the ends of the earth. . . .*

This gift of the gospel, this Good News, is entrusted to two different kinds of preachers.

One kind of preacher wants to provide his or her congregation with a *map* to go along with the Good News, a sort of Triple A guide for the spiritual journey. I recently came across a youth director's letter to the Episcopal Young Christians about their upcoming summer trip. He wrote: "Remember kids—no sex, no drugs, no alcohol, no loud music; this is a church trip." Granted, such rules are necessary, but our explanation of them often makes it sound as if the gospel is our chaperone!

And old Qoheleth scoffs and says, "*Hebel!*"

The other kind of preacher reminds me of a story my father would tell again and again in his years of Methodist sermonizing. He used it to illustrate the difference between belief and trust. As I grew older I thought it to be trite, but tonight it seems appropriate.

> *A traveling tightrope artist would go from town to town, stretch a line across a precipice, and gather a crowd. When everyone's attention was fixed on him, he would ask, "Who believes I can walk across this tightrope?"*
>
> *"I do, I do," they all would chorus back.*
>
> *So he would take his balancing beam and stride confidently out onto the line and over the chasm.*
>
> *Then, returning to the ledge, he would say, "Now who will climb up on my back and ride across with me?" Dead silence. No hands went up. They all believed he could do it, but they weren't willing to trust him enough to carry them.*

The second kind of preacher is a tightrope artist. You carry yourself—not *you* yourself, but the grace of Christ that is *in* you, the *earthen vessel* you, the you born of baptismal integrity—out onto the line stretched tense across the chasm. Taking hold of the balancing beam of Scripture, tradition, and reason, you glide out onto the wire and invite your congregation to ride with you across the gulf.

That moment is magic. It almost always happens out over the edge, on the precipice, over the pit. It is the moment when the Word Incarnate, who dwells in us, transforms us, and calls forth in us a new creation, a new being, a new world.

There you are where you do your best work, high above the bottomless vapor, with no net—your congregation balanced entirely upon your word.

And when you arrive at the middle of the divide, and everyone is holding his or her breath for fear of falling, that is when you dance! And then you sing at the top of your lungs a song that goes something like this:

For everything there is a season, and a time for every matter under heaven! And all times are God's times, and all is in God's hands, and Cephas and Paul and Apollos and Qoheleth and you and I, in Christ, are God's to use and God's to hold and God's to give.

I'm telling you, that's magic.

Qoheleth is not particularly impressed; but he does not scoff, and he does not laugh.

And you go to the door and the people come out of the church one by one and they speak to you:

"Good job, Padre . . ."

Thank you.

"Have you noticed that cobweb in the light fixture over the pulpit?"

No, I haven't.

"I have another fruit salad for you in . . ."

In the refrigerator in the kitchen, with my name on it. Thank you.

"I took the liberty to write this note about your Christmas sermon."

Thanks.

What are we to do with these people?

Well, we have two choices.

> *Joe G. Burnett is Professor of Pastoral Theology at the School of Theology, University of the South, Sewanee, Tennessee.*

---

1. Parker Palmer, *The Courage to Teach: Exploring the Inner Landscape of a Teacher's Life* (San Francisco: Jossey-Bass, 1988).

2. Galatians 1:6b–7a, 8.

3. Galatians 2:20.

PROPERS FOR SOCIAL JUSTICE

A Dangerous Vocation
James 2:5–9; Matthew 10:32–42
Debbie Metzgar

IT WAS a Wednesday afternoon at the parish when Roger's letter came from the Preaching Excellence office. I'd been eagerly awaiting its arrival, wanting to see when during this week I'd be preaching and exactly what the propers would be. I walked down the hallway of our church offices, tearing open the envelope as I went and scanning the first page.

"Nope. None of these times so far." I flipped to the second page. "Oh, there I am. The Thursday morning Eucharist. Oh, wow! They're the propers for social justice!" I smiled. "God is really good," I thought to myself. "Here's a topic I'm passionate about, and I've been handed a chance to preach about it to a great group of preachers. What a gift."

"Let's see. . . James as the Epistle. Now that'll be the stuff about not treating rich folks better than poor folks. And Matthew. That'll be the stuff near the end. The 'feed the hungry, clothe the naked, whoever-cares-for-the-least-of-these, cup-of-cold-water-to-a-little-one' stuff."

I sat down at my desk, pulled out my Bible and turned to Matthew 25. "Now. What's the exact passage? Wait. What? Matthew chapter *ten*? What on earth is *that*?" I flipped back to the earlier section and started scanning: "Whoever denies me, I will deny before my Father. I have come not to bring peace, but a sword. I've come to turn everybody and their aunts, uncles, cousins and in-laws against each other!"[1]

"Help! *This* is not what I expected! Who picked *these* as the propers for social justice?" I have to admit—there was cold water, all right, but it was much more a *douse* of cold water on my enthusiasm than a *cup* of cold water to "one of the least of these."

Some further reading showed that the disciples were at something of a preaching camp themselves. Jesus had been going around Galilee preaching powerful sermons (up on a mountain, it said). He'd been sending paralytics running home with their pallets, giving sight to the blind, and generally having a very successful-looking time of it. "*Never* before have we heard anything like this," the locals were saying.

And now Jesus has gathered his disciples around him. As his closest followers, they had been right beside him, watching him work, getting their training under their belts—and now he's about to send them out on their own. To send them out on a preaching mission, out to the various pulpits in their hometowns around Galilee, out to be preachers in a certain time and a certain place. Here in chapter ten, he's created a little training conference for them, a time to brush up on their homiletical skills, as it were. A chance to hear directly from him about what lies ahead, so they'll be ready. Perhaps you can imagine their excitement. "I wonder what pulpit I'll be sent to? I wonder how my sermons will be received? *You* know—what kinds of things the locals will *say* as they shake hands on their way out the door after services."

And what does Jesus tell them? What *can* they expect as preachers sent out in his name? What *can* they expect when they arrive to proclaim the gospel? When they climb up into a pulpit, take a sip of water (remembering always to be grateful to the altar guild), when they shuffle their carefully prepared pages, when they take a *deep* breath and launch into proclaiming the Word, what will the response be? "*Never* before have we heard anything like this. Oh, please— keep going. Tell us some more. We're all in our pews taking notes. We just *love* what you have to say to us."

Well, not *exactly*. Not according to Jesus. It's more like floggings, imprisonment, and alienation from those they love most. Crosses to pick up and the loss of their lives. Late night phone calls. "Thank you. I'll give him the message."[2] "What?" say the disciples. "Who picked these propers? What are you talking about, Jesus?"

It doesn't seem like the best of news. If it gave them pause, you can hardly blame them. If they *took* that deep breath, and climbed down *out* of the pulpit, perhaps you can understand. You'd have to be a little crazy, to sign on the dotted line for all of *that*.

If Jesus is right, a vocation to preaching is a dangerous thing. If Jesus is right, then maybe Roger ought to change around our conference T-shirts a bit. Instead of THE PREACHING EXCELLENCE CONFERENCE, maybe they ought to read THE DANGEROUS VOCATIONS CONFERENCE. Because if we do our jobs well—if we do, indeed, preach with excellence, then it sounds like Jesus is saying that we had better take a *big* sip of water and a *really* deep breath.

And here's at least part of the reason why. Because if we preach the gospel with integrity—if we do, indeed, climb into that pulpit to proclaim the arrival of God's reign—then we climb up there to proclaim that everything is up for grabs. That everything is different. That the world as we knew it has passed away and the radically new has arrived.

We need a big sip of water and a deep breath. Because to follow Christ—to preach the gospel—is to proclaim that all of the boundaries the world has taught us to draw, all the markers we have been taught to notice, all the distinctions between us we are so fond of making, all these have been proclaimed "null and void" by the God who makes us one. And who is busily at work tearing down the dividing walls that our world is so skilled at building up.

The dividing walls that *create* social injustice, that provide deferential treatment to the rich, that count things like skin color or language or sexual orientation as important distinctions when assigning worth—all these things have really got nothing at all to do with it, says Jesus. They're not what count—and woe betide to any of those who think they do! Those days are over—and the *truth* of it will be like a sword, cutting straight through the social arrangements that insist that such distinctions *do* count, that such markers *are* what's important to attend to.

It's just what James is saying to his community in the Epistle lesson. James's community had been putting the rich and powerful in the front pew, on the vestry—perhaps in their pulpit?—and he was sending them a bracing reminder that the distinctions they were making were based on all the wrong markers. James, and Jesus, are announcing that the markers that count are the ones given to us in baptism. That the distinctions that *do* count are the distinctions between those who join in with what God is up to in the world and those who do not, between those who acknowledge Jesus before others and those who do not.

Such announcements are dangerous proclamations to make. To preach in ways that don't simply *comfort the afflicted*, as Matthew 25 would have it, but in ways that *afflict the comfortable*, as Matthew 10 would have it—those are the ways of dangerous words, of words that challenge the status quo. That gets you marked as one who's moved "from preachin' to meddlin'," as they say. Those are words that need big sips and deep breaths when you step up into the pulpit.

And here's the Good News: If the gospel needs big sips and deep breaths to proclaim, big sips and deep breaths are just what you're given. Big sips provided, not by your reliable altar guild, but by your reliable Savior, who makes you marked, not as meddlers, but as Christ's own forever. Who pours out *rivers* of living water, which are more than enough to wet the dry mouth of even the most nervous of preachers. And the deep breaths that can calm nerves and provide courage are deep breaths of the very breath of God. Of the very Spirit who quickens in you the Word to proclaim.

So be prepared. Step into the pulpit and take a big sip—you'll find plenty to drink. Take a deep breath—and find it the breath of God. It's a vocation, this preaching life—and you'll find that it isn't so dangerous, after all.

Debbie Metzgar is Assistant Rector at
Holy Innocents Church, Atlanta, Georgia.

---

1. Matthew 10:33–35.

2. A reference to the conference presentation by Bishop Duncan Gray. When telephone threats came because of his stand on civil rights, his wife would always courteously respond with this phrase.

FEAST OF ST. BONIFACE

Do Not Shrink from Declaring

Acts 20:17–28; Luke 24:44–53
Hope H. Eakins

WELL, IT IS almost over. You have been instructed, exhorted, and inspired. You have been told that preaching is like martyrdom, like parachute jumping, and like playing in the attic. Now you are being sent out to do it, to preach God's mighty Word.

Where will your pulpit be and what will it look like? Pulpits, like sermons, you know, come in all styles and sizes. There are wobbly ambos that look like little more than frames for laundry baskets, and large stone podia with steps too steep for old preachers to climb. There are mobile pulpits that carry the likes of Roger Alling literally into the midst of God's people,[1] and pulpits so solid and firmly fixed that they convey authority by their very weight. There are pulpits with sounding boards like big clamshells that make us fear for the preacher's safety, and even bigger pulpits yet that hover over little altars to declare the primacy of word over sacrament. Some pulpits are like little roomettes that keep our wobbly knees from showing, and some are no more than rails that leave us nothing to hide behind. Sometimes aisles and chancel steps serve as pulpits. But while you are imagining where you want to plant *your* feet, remember that there are pulpits that do not live in church.

Surely no one could have taken the preaching endeavor more seriously than Paul, but Paul's preaching was not limited to the synagogue bema. Paul told the Ephesian elders, "I did not shrink from declaring to you anything that was profitable and from house to house."[2] Not only from house to house but in the amphitheater in Ephesus and in the forum in Athens, in the city streets of Lystra, in marketplaces, prison cells, and in Agrippa's throne room.

Paul preached wherever there were ears to hear, and so did Boniface whom we commemorate this day. Like Paul, Boniface had a passion for preaching the Good News to the corners of the earth. He refused his election as the abbot of an English monastery and set off to beg the pope for a chance to preach to the pagan nations instead. First to the solid citizens of German towns and then to the church in France (surely securing for all time the title Apostle to the Burghers and the Franks). Boniface's whole life was on the move, his whole zeal to evangelize those who were in the darkness.

That is God's call to every preacher, to proclaim the Good News to those in the darkness. Too often, I think, we limit preaching to what we do on Sunday morning, and we climb up into pulpits, forgetting that we are also called to climb down to preach in the streets.

There's a world out there that hasn't heard the Good News. "Thus it is written," said Jesus, "that the Christ should suffer and on the third day rise from the dead, and that repentance and the forgiveness of sins should be preached in his name to *all* nations beginning in Jerusalem."[3] The whole point of preaching, Jesus said, is to proclaim Good News to a world that has not heard it. And too often, far too often, the world never hears it because although the sermon begins in Jerusalem, it never leaves there.

I know a young man who . . . Well, to be honest, this is not a story about "a young man who" but a story about my son. I have chosen to tell it to you, to engage in this personal disclosure, because I want you to hear the story of a miracle in the happening. A miracle that cannot be completed until the gospel is preached in Cincinnati and proclaimed, not in a church pulpit, but in a pulpit such as Paul and Boniface used.

The story begins in the middle of the night last February, when I got a call that my thirty-one-year-old son Dan had suffered a severe heart attack from an overdose of drugs. He was in a deep coma, kept alive only by machines. We stood by his bedside for days until they said that there was no hope for his survival. So we called his brothers and asked them to fly to Cincinnati where we prepared to pull the plug and let Dan die in peace. But God had a different idea. As we prayed and cried our good-byes, Dan opened his eyes.

There was still no chance for a full recovery, they said; his coordination and mental function would always be compromised, and his kidneys were not working. But as it turned out, I saw Dan last week, and he has a job and an apartment and he cooked me meals. His coordination is fine, and he negotiated the complicated map of the Cincinnati Zoo better than I could. His recovery is a medical miracle, they say, and it is a spiritual miracle too, for he knows that it was the power of God that saved his body, and he is beginning to know that he needs the power of God to save him from addiction, too.

Last week, Dan pointed down the street from his apartment. "Do you know what that church is?" he asked, and I read the sign: NORWOOD WESLEYAN CHURCH. "It is a Methodist church," I said, and he asked me what Methodist churches were like. But when I launched into a lengthy speech about the Wesleys and their Anglican heritage, and hearts being strangely warmed, Dan interrupted me. "But what's it like? What do they do? Could I wear my jeans? I walked by last Sunday, but all the windows are stained glass, and I couldn't see inside the doors, and I couldn't get up the nerve to go in."

Now it will come as no surprise to you that my new passion is to replace all the heavy wood doors of our churches and to open all our windows so that the hymns and the preaching can pierce the air with their sounds of joy and hope. But short of that, I want to stir up in every preacher with a passion to preach in Christ's name, I want to stir up in *you* a passion to preach to the world beyond our church walls. And when we can't go there ourselves, our preaching must empower our congregations to go for us, to go for God.

We have spent this week studying and practicing homiletic skills. We have talked about delivery and content, and the use of story and the exegesis of Scripture, but all of those skills are important only if they are used to reach the ears of those who do not know Christ.

Have you read the book of Acts? Have you looked at those maps of Paul's missionary journeys? From Athens to Philippi to Thessalonica, across seas and mountains, from Miletus to Rhodes to Tyre to Jerusalem? Can you fathom Boniface's journey? From England to Rome to Bavaria to France? These were men filled with a passion to share the gospel. These were men whose heritage is ours.

Paul said to the elders, "I did not shrink from declaring to you anything that was profitable and from house to house." We cannot shrink from such declarations either. The Good News of God in Christ is news too good to keep for ourselves and too good to keep inside the church walls. We've got to go public; we've got to go from house to house.

Paul said that his life was of no value unless it testified to the gospel of the grace of God. As we have heard this week we do preach with our lives as well as with our words, with our choices and our passion and compassion, with our schedules and with our affections. But we must also always be prepared to give an account for the hope that is in us, wherever and whenever there are ears to hear, even if there is no time to read a commentary, to do fine exegesis, or to write a manuscript.

Therefore the Word of God must dwell in you richly. You must be steeped in the words of Holy Scripture so that you can speak God's Word into the needy places of this world. You must know the story by heart. Do not let your prayer life grow stale. Do not let your study become routine. Do not let your Bible become a paperweight for the church newsletter.

You *will* preach this day. Through your silence or through your words, you will preach to your roommate, to the man in the airplane seat next to you, to the kid who asks where you have been this week. Maybe, God forbid, given the way the planes fly around here, you'll get stranded in Cincinnati and see a young man looking through a church window. What will you preach to each and all of these?

"*Who is God?*" they may ask. Tell them that God is love so great as to make a world. *Then why is the world so loveless?* Well, that's because we got greedy and scared and thought there wouldn't be enough love to go around, so we tried to keep it for ourselves. *So what did God do about that?* Ah, God kept on loving us so much that God sent prophets to tell us that there was always enough love and when we didn't listen to them, God sent us a little baby to be born in a stable, and that baby gave his life that we might live. *But how can a baby give us life?* Well, that baby grew up and showed us that God's love is so great that even death couldn't conquer it, that God's love is so vast that no sin is beyond its saving embrace. *Well, then what's the church for?* Tell them the story of Mary and Priscilla and Paul and Boniface and Martin Luther and Martin Luther King Jr. and Roger Alling[4] and Gary Shilling. Tell them about God's people who are still moved by the Spirit to proclaim Good News to the poor and release to the captives and sight to the blind.

"I did not shrink from declaring to you anything that was profitable and from house to house." Ours is a story too good to be kept in the pulpit. Go and preach it with your lips and with your lives. Preach it standing tall in the pulpit and do not forget to bend down and preach it to the little ones in the street. Preach it crafted with all the scholarship and skill and imagination that are in you, but never forget to preach it also as a simple story from your heart.

Hope H. Eakins is Rector of St. John's Church, Essex, Connecticut.

---

1. A conference reference to a pulpit on wheels that moved whenever it was gripped and leaned on.

2. Acts 20:27.

3. Luke 24:46–47.

4. The President and the Chairman of the Board of the Episcopal Preaching Foundation, which underwrites the annual Preaching Excellence Program.